Silencing the Monster

JENNIFER HATTON

PAGE PUBLISHING, INC.
New York, NY

First originally published by Page Publishing, Inc. 2019

ISBN 978-1-64628-736-9 (Paperback)
ISBN 978-1-64628-737-6 (Digital)

Printed in the United States of America

Introduction

To any and all that read the contents of this book, it is *not* meant to hurt, punish, or condemn anyone in any way. This is my own true story and in my own words that are unfabricated and unembellished of growing up and not ever being professionally diagnosed or properly treated for the multiple mental illness diagnosis I have. Only at the age of eighteen did I find the strength, courage, and financial means, did I go on my own to seek the help and the support I should have gotten as a child but never did.

When I was a child, I had what we would refer to as stage one of a terminal disease that exists inside my mind. If treated, acknowledged, and supported, I might have had a great chance at a different life, a different outcome. But because eighteen years went by, and I was then at stage four—the last stage. Remission bordered on impossible. How my own parents, family, and the "system," we pay millions of dollars to and set in place, simply failed me. And because of it, it unleashed a domino effect that led me down a road of self-destruction, self-mutilation, and self-medication.

Every story has two sides, and people say, "Somewhere in the middle lies the truth." Whether it is my side or your side, it does not change the damage, devastation, or destruction of the actions, reactions, or no action at all of everyone around me that caused or allowed the pain to happen to me that I still endure today, but at a much greater level. And how it will forever be etched in my mind and carry it around with me in an invisible backpack that somedays becomes too heavy for my shoulders, and I breakdown and fall completely apart.

Regardless of whether it was done intentionally or out of ignorance, it really does not matter if the outcome is still the same. Perception is reality, and how I perceived it is real and so raw that it changed the course of my life that could have been different, but it is not and never will be. My story is meant to both heal myself and free me from the bondage of lies, secrets, shame, and not ever feeling that I measured up to what people refer to as "the normal society."

In any twelve-step program for recovery of any kind, their motto is all the same, "To thy own self be true." Which basically means if you're not going to be open and honest with anyone else, at the very least, be true to yourself. Lies and secrets are what keep people sick and even kill or destroy the person that carries them around. The day will inevitably come when the burden is so great that they then turn to substance abuse or suicide to numb out or eliminate the pain they feel inside their own heart and mind which they have carried inside them for years and cannot deal with it personally on their own, so they find a way to escape from it all temporarily or sometimes sadly forever. Only through intense therapy and the eighteen months I spent in a NAMI (National Alliance on Mental Illness) treatment program, did I learn that no matter what it costs you—mentally, physically, emotionally, or financially—always let the truth be known and face the core problem head-on, or it will snowball into something so huge you can no longer handle it on your own.

Through my own story, I not only free myself but I give a voice to someone else that suffers the same afflictions of mental illness, addiction, betrayal by loved ones, or all the above. Those that feel they are not strong enough to speak for themselves but instead live in the shadows and hide in the darkness of life because they feel no one understands them, there is no hope or place to turn to without being judged or locked up. How simple acts of kindness and true love for another human being always outweigh the presence of hate every time. The raw and ugly truth that people don't want to face is that there are millions of us all over the world that battle this everyday and suffer in silence.

According to NAMI, 43.8 million, or one in five Americans suffer from one or more mental illness diagnosis. The Center for

Disease Control reports that suicide is the tenth leading cause of death here in the United States alone and is rapidly rising. The statistics also say that every thirty seconds, someone attempts to take their own life. And sadly worldwide, eight hundred thousand were successful in these attempts. This is not only disturbing but is becoming a huge epidemic that we are now seeing not just on local news but on national news and especially among celebrities and their children.

The ironic thing is that mental illness and suicide is much like cancer; it does not discriminate in any way, shape, or form and does not care who you are, how much money you have, what kind of family you come from, or even how important you are in society. You don't choose it; it chooses you! The alarming fact is that 80 percent of all people who suffer from addictions of any kind also have some form of mental health issues or illness. When substance abusers die, they classify their death not as a slow suicide but by shamefully by labeling it "death by drug overdose" or "cirrhosis of the liver," or my favorite, "complications due to chronic alcohol or drug use." So the true statistic that is never really published is if you combine these deaths, with the worldwide suicide-labeled death rates, you actually get around almost four million people who died by their own choice and their hands just last year alone.

Whether it be over as fast as gunshot to the head or a slower suicide of alcoholism or prescription pain pill addiction that over years eventually destroys your organs, a death by your own intent is still a suicide and should be classified that way. Now is the time for all of society to finally wake up and look around you. See who is missing, who is lost, and see who is actually staring back at you in the mirror. If you change nothing, then why are you surprised that nothing has changed? The truly astonishing thing to me is that when someone you loved commits the ultimate act of internal torment and takes their life, people act or even say, "I had no idea!" That is a total lie to make. The other person still breathing in this life feel better about the choice they made—to ignore the signs, symptoms, and in some case, that person telling them to their face that they felt that way—but you chose to do nothing about it for whatever reason. The fact is that most people who do kill themselves do not leave a suicide letter behind not because they want it to be a mystery but because they spent months and sometimes years telling anyone who wouldn't listen and finally they had enough. They never left a note because they felt inside that they had already given the explanations over and over again and no one listened so why even bother telling them again. That is the disturbing reality of suicide.

I live every day of my life battling my suicidal mind. Somedays I feel I can make it. Other days I spend in the dark, by myself, and thinking of the best way to make my pain go away forever. This is my reality.

Only at my worst moments of insanity, do I find my most creativity.

—Jennifer Hatton

CHAPTER 1

The Monster in my Mind

There is a "Monster" that lives inside my mind and in the minds of millions of people all over the world. Some of which don't even know of his presence simply because he has been living there inside them since birth, and to those in which he dwells, most don't even know life without him. For others, he develops over time and grows like a cancerous tumor in your brain. Until the day comes when he has grown so large, that he completely takes over your life, and it is just like having stage four cancer, just too little and much too late. He comes like a thief in the night, rarely giving signs or notification that he is coming.

One day you just wake up, and he is there, like an uninvited friend or family member that shows up unannounced and knocks on your door with bags in hand and nowhere to go, so you let them stay. They say they just need a few days to figure things out, but they end up staying for months or even years in some cases. The longer they stay, the harder it is to get them to leave. But with The Monster, he comes only to kill, steal, and destroy everything in your life and the lives of the ones around you. He takes whatever he wants, whether you give it to him freely or not, and then he leaves unexpectedly. You never know when he will be back, but he always does return.

For some, The Monster has an audible voice that they truly hear. For others, like myself, he speaks to me through my thoughts, and his voice is actually my own. The message he brings is always the same: he is there to remind and convince me of all the wrong choices I have made in life—the irreversible pain I have caused others, how I will never amount to anything, and that I should just give up and end it all right now. He tells me that everyone in the world is against me and out to get me. The worst lie he tells is, "The God you believe in and pray to simply does not exist, and you are foolish to follow the word of this being you call the Almighty One. That you have never seen or actually truly heard the voice of." Then he says, "When I come, you can hear me loud and clear. You always do as I say, and if you don't, I remind you that I know the ugly truth about you. Therefore, I am real, and I do exist." With him, he always brings a cloud of darkness and sucks out every bit of energy, hope, and ambition I have.

I personally have tried to fight him ever since the day I was made aware that not everyone hears him and that it is not normal for him to speak to and control me. I tried to tell people about him when I was growing up as a kid, but no one believed me, or if they did, they were simply so scared of what I said that they then wanted nothing to do with me and told me to stay away from them or their children. They treated me, when I was just a child, as though I was possessed by the devil and was this "child of Satan" and that I didn't deserve to be paid attention. So I stopped talking about him just so I could belong and fit in among the family and to try to acquire friends.

I kept my feelings of hopelessness mostly to myself while I watched everyone around me live in joy and happiness, and in return hatred, bitterness and anger grew inside me. Only at the age of eighteen did I finally make the appointment, pay for myself, and go all alone to see a psychiatrist for the very first time in my life. I was terrified of what he would say or do when I told him about The Monster and my darkest days. I was afraid he too would look at me with fear and tell me I was a lost cause. Only then did I find out that I was not possessed by the devil and that I actually had a real illness that went untreated all this time. He told me I was not crazy or evil and that people who do not understand or have the knowledge of mental illness are often scared by it and chose to live in ignorance once they do find out.

The reality he told me was that this something that is not cur-able; something I will always have, and that since it is not an exact science to which you can see under a microscope or through an x-ray, it can change and morph into many diagnoses over the years. For me it was a double-edged sword; I had finally found out I have a true ill-ness, but that it is chronic and that there is no cure. From that point, I went on a roller coaster trying to fight The Monster off with anti-depressants, antipsychotic drugs, mood stabilizers, and prescription anxiety drugs as my weapons.

I thought to myself, *This time I can go back home and tell all my family that once judged and labeled me that I have a true and real disease*, and I believed they would react just like any other relative or friend who just got a diagnosis of cancer or diabetes. I truly thought that they would be sympathetic and loving. That they would ask, "What can we do help? What is the treatment plan? Or can we pray for you?" That was not at all the reaction and response I got.

I was excited and happy to finally know that what I had was a real medical condition and that I wasn't crazy or possessed; that I had hope now for a future and that many treatment options were available to me. For about an hour or two, a weight had been lifted from my shoulders that I could now say I had something real. I had outlook and faith that hadn't existed before. For the first time, I didn't think that suicide was my only option. Then it was stomped on and crushed as soon as I got home to tell my immediate family. I was told, and I quote, "You act like this is a good thing, that your happy to be told you got mental problems. It's like you wanna be just like your dad, crazy and medicated on these prescriptions. Don't you know, if people find out or they drug test you for a job, you won't ever have anything?" My feelings of happiness and joy, at that very moment, were crushed, and I retreated back into the darkness where no one could judge me.

This is the story of events in my life all in sequence—to how it all began, how it unfolded, unraveled, and how it all ended. One life is not more important than another; one disease does not deserve more sympathy or loving attention than someone else's. I never did do anything to catch or contract this illness, but it doesn't really matter if I did or not. Everyone in this world deserves the very same loving compassion and support to get through it. No one has the right to make a judgement call on whether you get the treatment you need, the support you desire, or if your disease is something that can be accepted by your family and if you're still allowed to be a part of that family because you have it.

For the longest time, I had no voice. I suffered in silence and hid in the shadows, so I felt I belonged or fit in. It may have costed me everything; but today I can tell my story, today I am free, and today I can hold my head up high. And now I speak for those who can't find their voice. I am not ashamed. I am not defeated. And the label you once put on me is the same label I will pull off and use it to cover your mouth while I speak. I no longer have to sit in silence while I am being told I am wrong for having thoughts, dreams, and aspirations that didn't fit into your "cookie-cutter" lifestyle. I will no longer let you take away from me the love, support, and treatment I deserved but did not get. And now, you will answer to a court and a judge much higher than anyone that exists on this earth for what you have done or failed to do for me. I know I am forgiven because I asked to be, but for you on the other hand, I would be very afraid and ashamed of your actions done against me all because I am different.

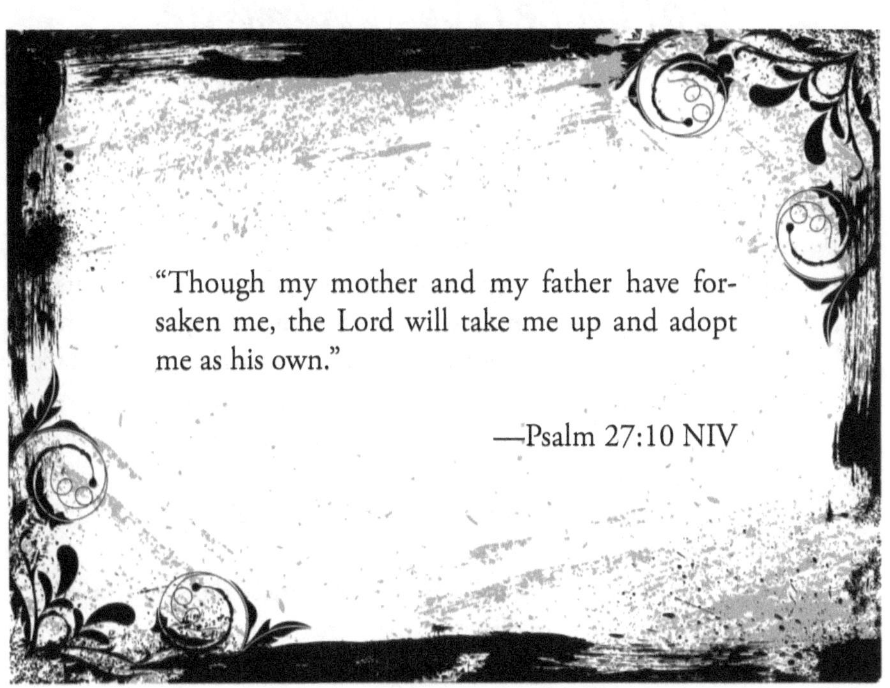

"Though my mother and my father have forsaken me, the Lord will take me up and adopt me as his own."

—Psalm 27:10 NIV

CHAPTER 2

Collateral Damage

The problem with today's world is that most people never think about the actions they take before they do them. They don't stop for a second to weigh out the repercussions their decisions will cause. In most cases, they don't even care at the time. They want what they want right now and do not think about tomorrow or the years down the road or how it might affect those around them. And even after the smoke clears, they still feel that it was not their fault they unleashed a domino effect that hurts or destroys the lives of others. They almost never take responsibility or admit their actions caused this kind of devastation.

We live in an instant-gratification world these days, and it will be the downfall of what is referred to as "the normal population of society." My question is: exactly who set the standard for what is normal and what is not? That is a question in which no one has ever answered.

The phrase "collateral damage" is loosely defined as "a term for death, injuries, and other damages done on an unintended target or innocent people." This term is mostly used in the military to describe the people, places, or things that were hurt, injured, damaged, or killed "accidently and unintendedly," while trying to destroy or take out the true targeted agenda. Nobody is ever held accountable, prosecuted, or reprimanded for these casualties and tragedies that unleash a ripple effect that change the course of all the lives involved. They are simply known as a fact that will happen in war of any kind. But what about when it happens in real everyday life to innocent victims, not in a designated war zone or military-driven battlefield? What about the average person or child that instead was born into it, or that the victim's only crime was that they made the mistake of trusting another human being?

Not a day goes by that I don't feel inside me that I was the result of the *collateral damage* that multiple people contributed to, but all started with the actions of only two individuals. I know for a fact that they never even thought of the consequences of their actions, but instead of taking responsibility and clean up the mess from "the war zone" they personally made, they thought it was okay to simply walk away and go on with their lives to pursue and find their own personal happiness in life and never give a second thought to what it had done to me.

The intended target in this case was to put an end to, kill, or destroy a marriage and a family life that should have never been in the first place. They never saw when bullets were flying and bombs were going off as I was standing there in the middle of it all at five years old. Once the dust settled and the war was over, the soldiers (my parents) on opposite sides both walked away with merely surface wounds. I, however, was caught in the crossfire and was mortally wounded. Part of me died the day the war ended, and in return, something new grew inside me. This is my true story of how the war began and the uprise of a new being was formed.

In November of 1979, I was born to a teenage mother and an undiagnosed, mentally ill twenty-year-old father. They were married after six weeks of knowing each other, and red flags were flying all over the place that maybe they personally didn't see themselves, but to the grown adults around them, they would have had to have been totally blind to claim they hadn't seen the signs, warnings, and bright red flags blowing in the wind.

My mother was still in high school at the time. They were just ignorant kids or young adults—whichever way you chose to see them as—that had now made a very bad and terrible choice that would later fall like a house built of cards. A house that I never asked to be born into. I know they both were just trying to escape their own personal hell of growing up and not knowing yet who they really were as individuals. But that still didn't give them a license to do what they did. Maybe the truth and the reasoning I now know behind both of them should be enough for me to get over how they unknowingly stacked the cards of the beginning my life against me, but for whatever reason, it's just not a good enough answer for me.

My mother had and still has an addiction to food to calm her nerves, ease her pain, or fill a void in her life that I still today do not know why or what the core root of her addiction is. But I do know that every addiction, whatever it may be, is just a way to self-medicate the true underlying problem. She claims she has a thyroid problem and takes medication to control it and has for decades. She also had a gastric bypass done many years ago that forced her to not be able to overeat, and in return, it made her lose around 150 lbs. or more. But the problem with that story is that scientifically, your body cannot intake any more food than what is needed to survive after the gastric bypass, and they physically cut out half of her stomach or more in efforts that she then will learn a routine of eating normal amounts of food and retrain this new behavior in her brain in order to maintain a healthy weight. That, coupled with the thyroid medication you take the rest of your life, should not make her mysteriously gain massive amounts of weight back and her to constantly keep fighting to lose it again. It is not medically possible that you can gain 50 lbs. or more in two or three months if you're not grossly overeating.

I have watched this battle of her addiction my whole life. What I still, to this day, don't know is why? What is she trying to avoid, dealing with, or running away from by self-medicating with food? Then lying about it or at least lying to herself and telling everyone it's her thyroid, slow metabolism, lack of exercise, or the job she works. I have heard it all over the years. But the reality is I know plenty of people who don't exercise, have a sit-down job, have thyroid issues, and eat garbage all day long, but none of them are or ever have reached morbid obesity. Every excuse given by her now is like a bell going off in my head saying "classic case of denial in addiction."

My father suffers from severe mental illness with multiple diagnoses. His family and himself, over the years, have told me that he showed early signs of something not being right with him. Like hallucinations, delusions, strange behaviors, and severe overreactions. Unfortunately, in the time when my dad was growing up, they did not have the knowledge, the progressive treatments, and wide assortment of medications they do today. He was never properly diagnosed, and treatment for him did not happen until the eighties, and even then, it was just the beginning stages of truly identifying and treating mental illness and not just locking up people in asylums and leaving them there to die.

With my mother, it's a mystery she hides. At least with my dad, he lays it all out on the table for me. And I don't live with unanswered questions. My dad tells me of a mentally, emotionally, sexually, and physically abusive upbringing. I don't know for sure that it happened exactly the way he tells it, but I see in his eyes and in his tears that on some level it did, and he still lives with the memories and flashbacks of it today. He can even tell me what year it was that it happened and even what the people were wearing that day, down to the color, type, and style of shoes they were wearing. He also told me that he was gay and that coming out with that was harder than facing the mental illness diagnosis. Following that, it to lead him down a road of self-medication with drugs and alcohol that almost immediately breeds addiction. But at least I know the core root of his issues. He, too, tells me about The Monster that lives inside his mind just like me. He may not have been there for me either, but at least, he admits he wasn't and he never tries to cover up the truth. And that the happiness he pursued after the war was over, he never found and he never did win the battle against The Monster either. My heart dies for him every time I still see him today, but I thank God at least he is still alive even though I know he wishes he was dead.

Anything can become an addiction to someone, but the key is hoping that person never finds what works for them in order to "not deal with the real issues behind the addiction." No one ever personally chooses to be an addict of anything! Just like no one wakes up and says, "Hey, you know what, I think today I will choose to lose my job, my car, my house, my family, my friends, and all my money just to become an alcoholic, a drug addict, or overeat to the point of morbid obesity just because that sounds fun!" It simply does not happen. Today I still cannot put a lot of the blame or even half of the blame for the collateral damage I was subjected to upon my father simply because, at least with him, I know and understand the underlying reason behind his behavior and actions. Living with lies and secrets are just like a wildfire; it all starts with one small, lit match, and if you do not do anything to put it out, it will continue to grow out of control and spread until it burns up everything and everyone around it.

The really funny thing is, for as long as I can remember from being a child all the way until today at thirty-nine, my father still breaks down, crying to me and honestly and wholeheartedly apologizes and begs me for my forgiveness about his part in my child and young adulthood which I continue to reassure him that I have forgiven him from the very first time he asked decades ago. But my mother, on the other hand, is a totally different story. She is the kind of person who says, "Don't rock the boat, don't stir the pot, sweep things under the rug, and pretend they are not there because if you no longer can physically see it, it does not exist." Those are all quotes she has said to me over the years in one way or another. As well as the implied but not spoken, "Shh…we don't talk about the elephant in the room. We pretend it's not really there so no one gets upset. Just leave it be, and that some secrets should always be kept and taken to your grave." She takes absolutely *no* responsibility whatsoever for the irreversible collateral damage done to me. Closure and peace I have begged her to give me; today I still have yet to see or hear, and I probably never will.

I believe it was around 1984 when my parents divorced. I was about five years old, and my mother was around twenty-three or twenty-four when we moved into a stable home with my grandparents and two uncles. I didn't see, hear from, or know much about my dad for almost a year or more. I asked about him, but I was told he lives in another town and works a lot and has a lot of things going on right now. The truth I found out years later was that he had his first clinical nervous breakdown after "the war had ended," and he was put into a mental hospital. I loved and identified with my dad, and every day that went by that I never heard from him or seen him, a piece of me died. I could relate, even at that early age, that we were a lot alike, and we had a special bond, and he was my hero.

One day he did start to come visit me and pick me. We had the best time; we went shopping and out to fancy restaurants, and he would turn the music up in the car so loud you couldn't hear anything else. It was him, singing eighties songs, and he danced in the car while driving. He did everything to make me feel special. He even bought me matching pair of boy's penny loafer shoes just like his, and we put pennies in them so we could match not only on the inside but on the outside. I didn't care that they were boys dress shoes. I just wanted to be like my dad. Then he would take me back to my grandparents and drop me off, and I would cry and stand in the driveway and watch him drive away and leave me behind. I died inside more every time I had to say goodbye. And I asked God why my daddy would leave me? What had I done to make him leave me behind? Again, silence from God, but The Monster spoke up loud and clear, and said, "Because you are not good enough or worthy of having a normal family life; with a mother and father that loved each other, and loved you all under the same roof, and you never will be."

Only when we become totally invisible, do we
finally see our true selves.

—Jennifer Hatton

CHAPTER 3

Little Girl Lost

It was thirty-four years ago when I was just five years old, but I still remember like it was yesterday. "The basement" of my grandparents' house—where my mother and I first moved to after her divorce from my father. It continues to amaze me how the mind can remember exact fine details, almost like a still photograph trapped inside your mind, about certain times or events in your life that happened decades earlier. But I cannot recall something simple like what I did last week.

There are things we see that later cannot be unseen and constantly play like a movie on auto repeat in our minds over and over again that we just can't turn off. Much like a soldier that comes back from war with visions of gruesome battles, voices with words that echo in our mind forever. There are situations where we are forced to go through as a child that write on the walls of who we will become later in life. Moments that happen in turn forever change you; turning points where once you cross over that line, you can never go back. Your childhood is simply the foundation that is being poured in order for you to build the rest of your life on. And if your foundation is unleveled, unfinished, or broken, then anything you try to build on top of it will not ever be right; and you will spend an eternity trying to "fix it" or "make it work."

Unlike a house, you can't just go and tear it down and rebuild on the same property. You can tear down walls of mistakes and build on additions of new hopes and dreams from what materials you have acquired yourself over time, but you only get one foundation that your life will dwell on. I remember this every time: "Turning point or point of no return." Depending how you perceive it, that happened to me as a child, an adolescent, and as an adult that changed forever who I was from that very moment. This is my story of being a "little girl lost," and not knowing where to find myself.

Today I am almost forty years old, but inside, I feel like I am still that five-year-old little girl that is lost and cannot be found, like I am frozen in time at the center point of where it all started to unravel. Growing up as a child in the eighties, there was no shortage of happy, unrealistic, family sitcom shows that portrayed a family dynamic that simply does not exist. The truth is that daddies do leave and mommies sometimes don't stay, and the ones you love most do turn their backs on you and do die by their hands or actions.

My mother began working a lot, even multiple jobs at some points. When she wasn't working, she was dating. She was only about twenty-four years old, and she thought she could just "start all over again" and not deal with the past mistakes she had made. She had the mentality, then and now, that if you act like something didn't happen or doesn't exist, then you don't have to deal with it. So she thought she could just go on and start herself a new "traditional-style" family life of her own, and I was just a box of memories of bad choices and mistakes that she had to drag around everywhere she went. That box you have and carry around, that you never reopen, but know its contents. That box of memories you take with you everywhere you move over decades—simply placing in the attic, top shelf of a closet, or in the garage; where dust collects on it, never revealing its contents. The only times at this age that I really remember seeing her or hearing her voice was when she sat and drank coffee and smoked cigarettes for hours either with my grandmother or her best friend from high school. I sat in the floor not too far away in the other room, and I never turned the lights on whether the sun was out or it was dark. These lights I could reach, but I felt more comfortable in the dark or with shade just sitting and playing with my dolls and listening to her "grown-up" conversations that she had no idea I was listening to.

It was like I did not exist. I started to slowly fade away. The Monster began to speak to me louder and on a more consistent basis. I did things to try to get her to notice me. I even remember going down to my grandparents' pool alone while she was having her coffee talk, and I held my breath and floated face down in the pool pretending to be dead. But she never noticed. I became invisible. Once in a while, if I was down there for like two hours, she would yell out the back door at me to make sure I was still alive. Little did she know, I was actually dead on the inside. The distance between us grew more and more every day. Everyone in the house was always so busy with work or school or dates or activities; it was like a tornado blew through every day, but I was still just sitting there.

My grandmother was a gentle and loving soul that I transferred my need for a real mother to her. My dad was MIA, so I transferred my want for a father to my Uncle David, who was fourteen years older than me; but I saw something in him, something that surrounded him, that I could identify with, but I was so young I did not understand what it was until it was too late. My God-given gift of seeing auras and an almost instant feeling of someone's true intensions, what kind of person they were and what was really going on inside their mind and souls. Most of the time, they didn't even know that much about themselves, but I did. I just never really spoke out about it until the last four years of my life. My grandfather worked third shift, and while everyone was out during the day, he came home and went to sleep and told me to stay inside this house and don't be pilfering through draws and messing with stuff, mind your business and play with your toys or watch TV. He was a man that grew up in "the Great Depression." He started working helping out his parents and siblings as soon as he could walk and talk. He was a quiet man that never showed affection, but I knew that was how he was raised. He was taught that you work all day, every day then go to bed and start all over again. That was his routine for eighty years. I, too, saw and felt something odd to me about him at the time, but I didn't quite know what is was until two years ago when all the puzzle pieces fit right into place.

So I, of course, did not do what he asked of me as a child when he was sleeping. I did whatever I wanted. Most of the time, he never knew what I was up to or had done. I just had to make sure whatever I was doing I was quite, because Lord knows you do not want to wake him up. It only took me one time to figure that out after he whipped me with a big, thick leather belt that had this huge buckle on it. He only got two swings in, for I managed to get away and go hide. After that day, I was quiet like a mouse. I also figured out that he could not hear anything I was doing if I went down to the basement. It was like 75 percent finished, and me and my mom's bedroom was down there. My playroom that I was allowed to keep all my toys in was the unfinished part with the HVAC unit and airducts. It had; junk with cobwebs in it, and it had two tiny windows. The light was one of those pull-cord lights that I couldn't reach the string to turn it on, so I just played down there most of the day with my toys and just the daylight that shined in from the tiny windows. It had concrete floors painted that were this weird brownish red color and was cold, so I brought my blanket in there to sit on. I played down there for hours by myself every day with my toys, my pretend friends, and a voice inside my mind. Until people started coming home, and I was no longer the cause of the noise to wake up my grandpa, so then I moved upstairs to try to be a part of things.

You never really miss the light of day until you have sat in the dark for years. You never appreciate a human life until it is gone forever. That basement became my "safe place." It was just me, my toys, and my disease. I never knew or thought I was special. I didn't understand why other kids got to live with both parents and siblings that paid attention to them and were always there looking over your shoulder and encouraging you to do and be better. I thought to myself at that time, *Better than what?* I had heard of this concept of being and doing better than you are today but knew nothing about it. The only people that really ever played with me were my Grandmother Ruth and my Uncle David when they had time between their busy lives.

I saw outside the neighborhood kids playing from the window in the dining room. So I asked my grandmother for a bike, and she took me to buy one. I thought if I had a bike, I could ride around the cul-de-sac we lived in and pass by those kids, and if they said something to me, I would stop, but if they ignored me, I could just keep riding. And that was exactly what I did. After a couple of times, they did ask if I wanted to play with them. They even asked if I wanted to come inside their houses and play and eat cause their moms were home and would fix us snacks while we played. Unfortunately, I had no real social skills, and I didn't know they did not have the one I call The Monster that spoke to them inside their minds. I thought everyone heard him. So after a few times, they stopped asking me to come over. And I would ride my bike past them again until I overheard them say, "Stay away from her. She is really weird." Once I heard that, I rode my bike home, back into the garage, parked it, and never rode it again; and I went back down to the basement where I was safe from judgment and rejection from the outside world so that now all I had to deal with was the normal rejection of the ones living inside the place I called home.

I felt invisible most of the time. And when I wasn't in the basement, I sat under the formal dining room table with a fancy cloth over it and played with a few toys I brought from downstairs and listened to what everyone else was doing and talking about. The next Christmas I asked for a little, pink radio that also plays and records on cassette tapes. I used the radio not to listen to music but to record my own voice and play it back, so I had my very own friend I could talk to and play with, and she responded back to me just by me pressing the play button. No one ever knew I did that. It was just a secret between me, The Monster, and my pretend friend on cassette tape, that now had a voice, my own voice.

My Grandmother Ruth took on the role of being my mother. She was a kind, gentle soul. In many ways, I knew she saw my pain, my sadness, and my feelings of abandonment. She never said anything to me about it, but I did hide around the corner and listen to her scold my mother for how I was being done by her. My mother, still an immature child posing as an adult, would raise her voice back at my grandmother and try to tell her she knew what she was doing and to not tell her how to raise her child or live her life. My grandmother; much like myself, I discovered decades later, would get right up in my mother's face with her finger pointed at her and say, "You listen here, I don't give a damn if you get pissed off or not. The truth is the truth, whether you wanna hear it or not. Wrong is still wrong, and while I still walk this earth, you're gonna listen to what I have to say."

Still to this day, my mother denies any neglect whether it be verbal, mental, or emotional abuse that happened to me and how I showed obvious signs of mental illness and pretended she did not see it until I was twelve or thirteen, and another family member saw and told her of the self-mutilation I was doing to my arms with knives and razor blades. She was not sympathetic or showed loving concern when she addressed it with me because she was now forced to do something about it since "the cat was now out of the bag." To most people, intentionally cutting your arms to hell with sharp objects till blood drips down is a cry for help or a cry for you to at least notice me, but to her, it was an embarrassment. She grabbed my arms pulled up both sleeves and saw what I had done both fresh and old, and she yanked me to the side and said, "What the hell are you trying to do? You are making me look bad in front of the family. Now everyone will know about your personal problems that are not my fault. I have your toddler half-sister and my marriage to your stepfather to worry about and take care of, and I don't need you pulling this crap." My hatred for her grew stronger every day.

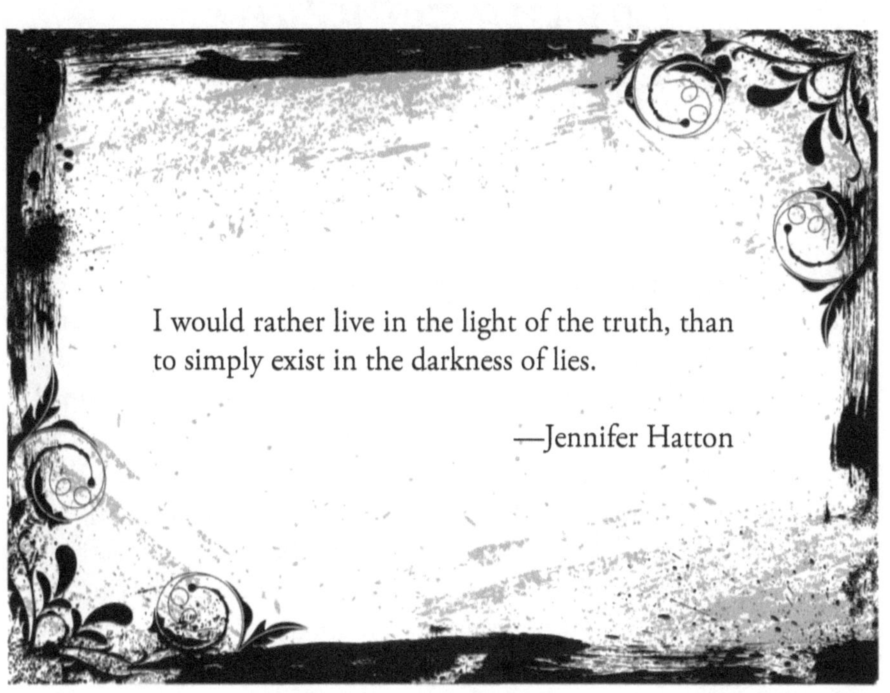
I would rather live in the light of the truth, than to simply exist in the darkness of lies.

—Jennifer Hatton

CHAPTER 4

Loving Someone from a Distance

When most people talk about the love they have for another, the person they are speaking to believes they are referring to someone that is present in their life at that moment. But that is not always the case. For me, I have had to learn to love many people from either a small or great distance away for many years, even decades. I suffered in silence most of the time and didn't elaborate on whether these people are alive or dead or if I had even seen or talked to them physically in months or years. I speak about them as though they are actively present in my life today because in my heart, they are, but in my mind, I know better. I keep waiting, thinking, and hoping that one day, they will come back, sometimes even from the grave; but so far, they have not. But today I still keep that torch burning and the light on outside my front door, thinking they might come back even in the middle of the night. These people include, but are not limited to the list that instantly pops into my mind, my mother, my father, my stepfather, my son, my daughter, my grandmother, grandfather, uncle, and sister. I truly love all these people but just from a distance.

The distance of the ones that devastate me the most are my two children. I have learned, over the years and in therapy, that the others I listed besides my kids probably will never come back and that three of them definitely will not because they are dead. The three I speak of died by a form of suicide and chose to leave this world forever by their very own hands and not the hands of the God Almighty. My children upset me the most because they are not adults yet and are very impressionable. My son will be eighteen this year and just recently he did not want to be a part of my life anymore based solely on his own abandonment issues with me as well as what has been and still told to him to this very day about me and over the past years that is one-sided and that everyone involved uses the openly known fact of my medically diagnosed mental illness and addiction problems as evidence to back it up. However, none of them even bothered to ask me how I truly feel inside, why I would overreact to a situation that involved them, or one that they only heard about through gossip and telltale story, sometimes even second or even third hand.

I cannot speak for anyone else, but personally I believe that God does not create people with hatred, jealousy, and anger inside them when they are born. Those emotions, feelings, and actions are learned or acquired behavior. I can also tell you when I see someone or anyone hurting inside or out, whether I know them or not. I open my heart, my door, and both ears to truly listen to what they have to say. Instead of just assuming they are crazy or some kind of a junky, alcoholic, or criminal—especially if I have never really had an in-depth conversation with them before. I always make it a personal rule to assume nothing. I would also *never* tell a little kid or teenager growing up that his or her own mother is completely crazy in everything she does. That statement you say to that child plants a seed in their little minds that their mother didn't want them, doesn't care about them, and is a liar because of it. What gives you or any human the right to sabotage a mother's relationship and bond with her own child? How can you claim to be a good God-fearing person and still think that was a good idea? Then, in return, you feel like you got to reprimand or punish me for anything you thought I did against you. I got some eye-opening news of revelation for you! You are *not* God. You are not anything besides a human being just like myself. And if you think, for one second, that your money, house, or status in this life gives you the right to make accusations upon me or my life, you are dead wrong; and I will pray on your judgment day that the good

Lord will show you mercy for thinking you had the right to do his job.

Another great personal tip for you is never say that those diagnosed with mental illness of any kind are "crazy." That is just an ignorant statement that now has become a label used by those claiming to be "normal." Just like the many ignorant statements in this whole world since the beginning of time, people had said and claimed about a group of society in order to punish, reprimand, and humiliate them. Like these words that are not limited to but include "faggot, nigger, raghead, and redneck," those labels were branded on people that have the same blood running through their veins as you do, but those words destroyed millions of lives that no one had the right to do! The best analogy I can think of is this. It's like there are thousands of little Adolf Hitler's walking around today, just trying to kill, persecute, and condemn those that are not just like them. Therefore, instead of doing the right and intelligent thing and try to understand why people make different choices than they would, live a different lifestyle, said or did something, they would not; they decide to make it their own personal mission, based solely on their own childlike insecurities and internal fears of the unknown; they produce hatred, judgement, and a punishment of their choice! Just because you don't like them for whatever stupid reason, or people don't live by the same rules you do, does not mean they are wrong, nor does it mean that you are right! My question then to you would be, "What gives you the right to judge me or anyone else on this earth for any reason?" And since you are now playing judge, jury, and Jesus Christ, you then go ahead and convict and sentence me in a court of law that you think exists inside yourself without even a trial or knowing all the facts behind the case. Assumption does not equal guilt. Assumption equals stupidity! So why don't you take an inventory of you own life and be judge and jury of your own train wreck before you start talking about mine? Which God or political government figure or party gave you the title of "Judge," and then handed you a black robe with a gavel? News flash: no one did! If that was all true, in your mind or your little ignorant world, wouldn't that make you exactly what your accusing me of? You labeled me as "crazy and a liar." So let me get this straight. I never once said or believed, for one second, that I was anything or anyone besides human. Nor did I or would I ever be self-appointed political party leader, judge, or play God. In my mind, that makes you "crazy and a liar!"

Today my seventeen-year-old son won't even listen to my side of the story, much less pick up the phone or respond to a text. Because in his young mind, it has been flooded over the years with lies and twisted truths from adults around him. My eight-and-a-half-year-old daughter even started asking questions in the last year or so, "Why did my mommy leave me?" I told her I didn't leave her by choice, but the people that are physically present in her daily life tell her different, and she has no reason at this age to believe me or want to search for the truth. I can tell you honestly that the loss of my two children at age two years old and at six months old was and still is to date the most devastating and painful thing I have ever went through. Even though it has been many years ago now, if I think about it too long, I open the door for The Monster to come in and tell me that, "There is no reason for you to even try to be in their lives. They don't want you to contact them. They are doing very well with their fathers and stepmothers raising them, and you are not even a memory any longer. My advice to you is do them both a favor and leave this world! They don't want or need you anymore, and all you are doing is causing them pain and confusion. You were never good enough to be a mother to them, and that is why God let them take the both of them away at such young ages. You don't get second chances in this life to be the mother you were not, so do them and the world a final act of justice and closure and leave this life on your own terms. It's the only thing you can do now." So I have had to learn not to think about it much anymore because I already know what will happen if I dwell on it. I hope that, someday, both my children read this and truly understand what I am saying to them.

If I could talk to them both as mature adults not at eighteen or even nineteen, I said mature, I would say this: To both Christopher and Kaitlyn, I love you both more than life itself. I would give anything to have the opportunity to raise you and be there on a daily basis. Today and always while I am still on this earth, I would give you anything I have including any material items as well as any organ in my body if it would save you or make you happy. My personal beef with either of your fathers is dead and gone, and I wish them both the best in this life. If you only knew of the psychological hell I went through, hearing multiple lawyers and judges across four states tell me the same thing, "You would have had a better chance of getting custody of either of your children if you had committed a felony, went to prison, did your time, and then went through a rehab program for hardcore drug abuse and graduated rather than the actual truth of having a clean record, a good job, no drug problem, having a diagnosis of any mental illness issues and a drinking problem induced by stress, abandonment, and betrayal." The funny thing is, the court cares nothing about the alcoholism; because they told me. I only developed it after my second baby was taken. They told me right out in the open in court they considered any mental illness diagnoses as a "chronic disorder" and that there is no cure, and they considered me to be high risk and they can't trust that I will take my meds and see my psychiatrist and therapist on a regular basis and that the court does not have the funds to monitor this; therefore, in both cases, their fathers were awarded joint custody with primary residency and were allowed to move anywhere they wanted to in the US, and I could not do a damn thing about it.

I spent tens of thousands of dollars, and had like three total nervous breakdowns requiring hospitalizations over you both. I also went to jail three times over two assault charges and one charge of alcohol intoxication because I was not going to let my third husband; I wrongfully married, slap me in the face, steal my money, and sell my medication and anything I had of value and threaten me! And yes, I was drinking inside my own home where I thought I was in my "safe place," but apparently it is not okay in the eyes of the law to spend your days off from work inside your own home and drink your pain and sorrows away and physically fight back when he hit me first because he was addicted to crack and cocaine, among other drugs, and he thought I should pay for his drug habits and dealer debts, and I didn't! It was then that he became so desperate for money and drugs that he hit me and I responded like "Oh, hell no," and I beat his ass and sprayed him with mace. Luckily it turned out to be a blessing in disguise. I was offered jail time of seven months or a new diversion court program that you are in for a minimum of one year and up to five years which was called "Mental Health Court."

It is only offered to people who were previously diagnosed with mental health issues before they broke the law. I have to say the first six months were hell on earth, but then something changed inside me. The judge and the panel of experts *never* gave up on me, which of course was new to me. The Monster came out and showed his face to everyone, and they beat him down until he was weak and I was stronger than him. It changed the entire game of life for me. I didn't think anyone could beat the Monster! And as of December 5, 2016, my charges were completely expunged, never to be found again, and I graduated the program with honors after eighteen months. I was the first dually diagnosed person to ever graduate MHC program. My dear, Katie, I lost you as just a six-month-old baby, and Christopher was about nine years old when I totally lost my mind and people started turning their backs on me like everything was my fault. Some people showed concern for a short while until it was obvious that I had become a full-blown alcoholic and displayed erratic behavior. Then they dropped one by one like flies, till they were all gone. They had never experienced what I actually went through; therefore, they had the "just get over it and move on attitude." Some even physically told me that. Well, what I say and still stand behind today is this: Whenever you have lost both your kids for a stupid ass reason, had three failed marriages, and at the same time, had lost not only your kids, husbands, your house, car, job, all the money you had, relation-ships with your family and so-called "friends," and diagnosed with four different mental illnesses, I am pretty damn sure you or any human alive would develop some kind of addiction to numb out the devastation you felt on a daily basis.

I consider myself lucky that it was alcohol instead of drugs or gambling. I guess because alcoholics were accepted in society, but drug users and gambling away tens of thousands of dollars were not. Even though I know now that we are all equal in addiction, no mat-ter what it is, I would like to say to both my kids that I am truly sorry for not being the mother you wanted or needed. I am also sorry that, in your heart and in your mind, you think I abandoned you both by choice, but I did not do so willingly. Nor did I not go down without an ugly fight, kicking and screaming. I would also like to apologize for the marriages and failed relationships I had with men that never worked out due to that fact that most were total losers that I chose myself. I apologize for any and all scenes or embarrassment I personally caused due to pain, resentment, and bitterness I had inside me. But what I will not apologize for is having mental illnesses because that is just like having a diagnosis of diabetes or cancer; I did nothing wrong to deserve it. Unfortunately I was born that way and did not get real help until I was eighteen years of age and paid for it all by myself. I did my very best to keep on top of my mental health issues through the years. I even chose to participate in a court program they offered me sponsored by NAMI instead of taking the jail time after the arrests that I was sentenced to. But after spending eighteen months in that program, I graduated on December 5, 2016. Then I divorced that loser and finally found a man that actually fought for me! He is a true and genuine person that has all positive things going for him and a heart of gold. Only by God's grace are we still together today because he walked into my life at my lowest point. I would also tell you that no amount of alcohol, medications, or therapeutic treatments can or would make it that could I forget about you or make the pain of losing you both any less today as it was when you were taken away. I will always have my door open and my light on waiting for one day that you might come home to me.

My children are not the only people I have learned to "love from a distance," but today, they are the most painful. Still the same, I continue to hold a torch for my mother, my father, stepfather, sister, and the three people that are no longer in this world—my grandmother, grandfather, and my dear uncle. I would have to say that hands down, I mourn those that have passed on the most after my children simply because I know for a fact I will never see or hear from them again on this earth. My father has always been special to me. I have always identified and saw myself in him and him in me. I could look at him and feel the pain he was feeling in his mind and heart, even with him saying nothing at all. I love him today from a distance not because he hasn't apologized over and over again, because he has, but because even today, I make unrealistic expectations of him, and I try to get close to him as my father and there is an invisible fence he put up and installed himself decades ago that I simply can't tear down; and trust me, I have tried many times.

My mother is another story. She has never once given me a true, heartfelt apology, just some pitiful, forced, and not genuine apology of saying, "I am sorry for whatever you think or believe I did even though I am innocent and did nothing at all to you." Does that really sound or feel like an apology to you? Nor has she tried to make amends to me. And the funny thing is she truly is baffled as to why I keep bringing up the past? Do you need me to rent a plane and write it in the sky for you? Or should rent a giant billboard and put it in the center of Pikeville? For such an intelligent woman, you sure are stupid when it comes to seeing what I really want and need from you; and it's not money or credit. It's a simple, damn, heartfelt apology with none of this bullshit of "whatever you think I have done, but I just have to tell you I did nothing." You know what that is called in a court of law? The legal term for it is an "Alfred Plea."

An Alfred Plea is when you will make a deal in the court system to avoid a trial and a take a shorter sentence based on saying you will agree to do the jail or prison time, but you admit no guilt. It's a bunch of horse shit if you ask me. I only believe in black or white, no gray area in the middle. Wow, that's it. All I ever wanted from you was closure, and I feel I can't get closure if I don't get a real apology, and then I can bury it and move on. I don't know why you won't give me that simple thing. I understand that you probably never intended on hurting me, but the fact is you did, and you are not on trial. I am constantly with the world of public opinion. Get over yourself and find a little humility. I can even let you borrow some of mine if you want. I got plenty humility stocked up to spread around and finally make the right damn choice!

To my stepfather and sister, there is little blame I place on you simply because you are victim to one of the oldest games ever played, which is the game of being hustled. Your hearts are good, pure, and in the right place, but I don't know where in the hell your brain is? Obviously, I have reached out multiple times to both of you, and you have listened but done almost nothing about it all because you have fallen victim to the "hustle," a psychological game of manipulation by one or more people that are active in your daily life, and they convince you of falsehoods that they want you to believe in the benefit of their behalf by even crying, yelling, and screaming to frighten you or make you feel bad enough that you feel threatened and imply that they might terminate any type of relationship with you if you do not take their side. And when your put in that scary position, you both fold even though you knew in your mind that I was right, but you were too afraid to take the gamble and stood your ground. I know secretly you admire my braveness, boldness, and the fact that I address a problem head-on and immediately when I see or hear of it, and I don't let it go until it is solved and corrected to be right at whatever cost I have to pay or who I have to go up against big or small to complete it. I truly do love you both, and because of that, I am telling you to stop being a doormat, and if someone is gonna take something from you or leave you because you challenge them, I got bad news for you: they are going to take or leave no matter what you do; so why live in the shadows and try to play both sides when you know you are right and then live with the guilt of "what you should have done?" Regardless, you are both beautiful souls, and we all three know the truth even if you're not brave enough to say it. Don't worry, I am brave enough for us all.

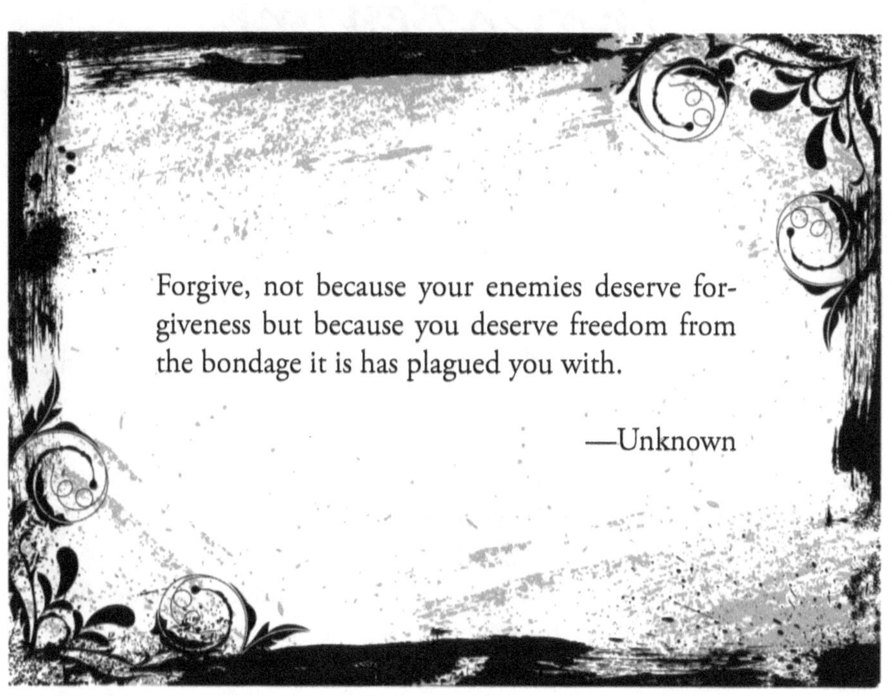
Forgive, not because your enemies deserve for-
giveness but because you deserve freedom from
the bondage it is has plagued you with.

—Unknown

The Chosen One

Bitterness is a dish best served cold. This particular chapter in my life is what I would call "my darkest years with the devil himself." That is why I often envy those that are ignorant and walk through life wearing rose-colored glasses. Those that are totally oblivious to reality. Those that when the music stops, they just keep dancing. The fantasy of a man on a white horse sent from God to rescue you and then you both ride off happily ever after into the sunset. That is what I thought my second husband was. He has told me and others countless times that he is "the chosen one." My response then is the same as it is now, "Chosen for what?"

What I did find out was that the devil himself truly does walk among us right here on this earth and that he can come in any shape, form, or disguise as necessary to bait you into his lies and manipulations. Satan will never come to you dressed as the devil; he will come disguised as an angel knocking on your door, waiting for you to open it and let him in. But when you invite him in, it will be the worst possible thing you could have ever done, and you will soon find out that getting him out will take an act of God to remove him. This is my experience with pure evil coming into my life masked as a religious Jewish man from Israel calling himself the chosen one.

According to man's law here on earth, "murder" is defined as: "the unlawful premeditated killing of one human being by another." What they are referring to is a human body that is no longer alive, that has no breath or heartbeat. Every day in this world, people are convicted of this crime and sentenced to life in prison or possibly given the death penalty. There is no statute of limitations on murder. It could have been yesterday or seventy years ago, but you can still be tried and sentenced at any age and at any time. The strange thing is if you murder someone mentally, emotionally, or spiritually, you are never held accountable by any court of law, never put on trial, or never required any sentence of punishment or restitution to the one you killed inside.

I personally would have rather be murdered physically than what was done to me over the years and finished off completely by the chosen one. The death of my spirit I still walk around with today, an empty black hole that nothing fills it. Physically I am alive, but I have actually been dead for years on the inside. I am a dead man walking. How is that okay? How is that legal I ask? The response I get from people, including the few family members I have left, friends, loved ones, attorney's, therapists, and my psychiatrist, is basically all the same, "I don't know. That is just the way the law works." Well, that answer is not good enough for me, and it shouldn't be for anyone else either.

I see people win lawsuits of millions of dollars every day for stupid shit! For example, just because you go to a fast-food restaurant, order hot coffee, and you spill it on yourself or burn your tongue, why do you think you deserve any money or a formal legal apology from the company you bought it from? You did *not* order iced coffee. You knew it would be hot; therefore, you don't deserve anything except what you paid for—which is the hot coffee. But apparently in a court of law, you do. I would have rather been set on fire and burned alive than what had happened to me, and I actually survived to tell about it.

To wake up every day knowing that others around me knew exactly what was happening, and they did little or nothing at all to help me. I personally told them, and they simply chose to just turn a blind eye and walk away because it was either too painful for them to hear, too much drama for them to want to be involved in, or they simply just did not give a damn. In my eyes, that makes you an accomplice to my murder. Which if I was killed physically, they would be held to the same standards of punishment as the murderer themselves in our justice system today, which our justice system is a total joke if ask me. The hundreds of thousands of dollars I have personally paid in to our government, not one time has it ever turned out to actually help me regardless of the solid proof and evidence I brought forth, never. If you personally saw, knew, participated, or covered up the death of another person and did anything to stop it, in no way helped the victim, or even worse, helped in the act, then you are just as guilty as the other person who committed the crime directly. However, because I was slaughtered to death on the inside, I unfortunately will never see justice on this earth, and I will never be given back all that I have lost because of it. But those that stood by and did not want to hear or see my cries for help, went on and lived their happy little lives while I rotted and died the second death in my own home. My first death I experienced as a child and a teenager from being different and being discarded like I was worth nothing, like I was trash to be thrown away.

I met the chosen one in 2003. That was a time in my life when I was married to my son's father, and I felt trapped not because he was a bad person but because I knew I had made a mistake and let family members, mostly my mother, talk me into all the reasons why I had to marry him. Those reasons really boiled down to the following: I had my baby son with him, no college degree, no means to support him on my own, and it is simply what you had to do when you find yourself pregnant and alone with no real career or money. I let my feelings be known that I did not want to get married, but because I was young and naïve, I did what they told to me because I felt I had no other choice, and I was too weak on the inside to go out on my own and fly free like I truly wanted. I think, deep down, my son's father didn't want to marry me either; he just probably thought the same things too. So after two and a half year, I knew for sure I wanted a divorce and go our separate ways, but I had no means or plans to make that happen. I never meant to hurt my son or his father, but I know I did. I also didn't know that divorcing him meant I would also lose my firstborn child. Those are regrets and pains I live with still today that still haunt me inside my mind and what's left of the heart I have.

The chosen one worked in the mall right across from the store I was employed at. It was not an immediate thing. It started with hi and hello and how are you today that led to hugs and gifts and long talks about ourselves. Then one day, everything changed when he kissed me on the cheek, and I felt electricity went through my body. He told me he loved me, told me he would give me the world and take care of me and my son as his own. So I fell hook, line, and sinker. I packed up my personal stuff and left my husband for him. I don't think I ever really gave a heartfelt apology to my son's father for leaving. But I want him to know today how truly sorry I am for whatever pain or hard times I caused him and my baby boy and to let my ex know that I got paid back a thousand times worse than I ever caused him and our son.

We should have never married in the first place, but my son, *I do not* regret for one second of having that tiny angel that is now an adult man who hates me. I admit that I let this man convince me to leave it all behind and move on to the world he was going to show me. I should have noticed the red flags that appeared in the first two months of us living together, but I believed him because he said, and I quote, "I am an Israeli Jewish man, and my last name is the same as Moses from The Old Testament in the Bible. I am a descendant of Moses." He said the Jewish people are the chosen people that will lead you to God. The scriptures that back that up is Exodus 19:3–6: "Then Moses went up to God, and the Lord called to him from the mountain and said, 'This is what you are to say to the descendants of Jacob and what you are to tell the people of Israel, "You yourselves have seen what I did to Egypt, and how I how I carried you on eagle's wings and brought you to myself. Now if you obey me fully and keep my covenant, then out of all nations you will be my treasured possession. Although the whole earth is mine, you will be for me a kingdom of priests and a holy nation." These are the words you are to speak to the Israelites.'" And my personal favorite he referred to was Zechariah 8:23, "This is what the Lord Almighty says, 'In those days, ten people from all languages and nations will take firm hold of one Jew by the hem of his robe and say, "Let us go with you because we have heard that God is with you."'" I thought to myself and said, *Why would I not believe him? These scriptures are not his own, but are of The Bible and are God's words.* That is how I justified my belief in him instead of the reality of what I was seeing with my own eyes.

My eye's showed me a notice on his apartment door; where I was living at the time, saying he was being evicted for two months of non-payment of rent. So I rushed down to the office to pay all the back rent and late fees that he said was a mistake on the apartment complex's part. But it wasn't true. The mistake was that I wanted to believe him; I wanted to be rescued by this holy miracle he was promising. Then a couple more weeks went by, and a knock at the door was heard by a rental furniture company coming to repossess all the furniture and the computers. Then he told me his business partner rented all that and the agreement was he was to pay that part but did not. So once again, I went out and bought outright, with my own money, furniture and a computer. Then about three weeks later, he said we have to move out of Florida, his business with his partner has gone bankrupt, and we have to move to Connecticut because he has a great job offer there with an Israeli-owned company. He couldn't get a regular job with an American company because he is only here on a tourist visa and has no green card, work permit, or social security number. Once again, a bright red flag flying high in the wind. At the time, my divorce had been finalized, and my son's father had no real family to count on or support him, so he told me he wanted my son to have a better life and to be close to relatives which turned out to be my own personal family he was referring to in Kentucky. My father had always lived there. My mother, stepfather, sister, grandfather, and uncle were already making plans to go back home to Kentucky and sell their properties in Florida. So once again, I felt I had no choice. But the truth was that I didn't know or see coming that I would be letting go of something I would never get back ever again. But unfortunately, we don't get a second chance at being a parent to the same child. We don't get another opportunity to see our babies grow up. All we get, if we are lucky, is a box full of pictures and hand-colored drawings done by a child you forever treasure inside your heart.

The chosen one made empty promises to me that if I followed and supported him in every way, I would get my son and we would be reunited and be a family. It was all lies. He didn't really work at all for two years. During that time, I worked two to three jobs just to keep us afloat in the ghetto, while he sat in his underwear all day and night, talking online to his friends and family back in Israel. I did my best to hold it all together, including my tormented mind, all the jobs I had to work, pay out all the bills, and scrape up enough money to fill out and file all by myself immigration paperwork so he could get legal status here. We could not afford a lawyer or even a paralegal to help me fill out three and half inches of legal paperwork and documents that I had no idea what I was doing. I had three nervous breakdowns over four months trying to do it all on my own. I even threatened to throw him out if he didn't do something, anything to help me bring money in, to take some pressure and stress off me. Again, empty promises and empty pockets. Since I could barely make the bills and our living expenses, I was forced to make the ultimate sacrifice and answer an ad to donate my eggs for $2,500. I needed almost $3,000 to file all the documents required to apply for legal resident status so he could get a work permit, a social, and a green card. I donated three separate times.

Finally, he did get a work permit and a social. The green card interview would be six months to a year down the road from that. I thought, *Thank God, he can finally get some kind of job, any job to help us.* He made one excuse after another, after another. I hit my breaking point. I moved out to an efficiency apartment in the nastiest, trashiest part of Cincinnati, Ohio, and told him "go make it on your own now. I am mentally and physically broken down, and I don't give a damn about you and your bullshit promises any longer!" So he mysteriously, all the sudden, got a job offer in Atlanta, Georgia, working for an Israeli company cleaning carpets for cash, no taxes. I said, "Whatever. Go, I don't care anymore." I lived in that trash hole with crackheads in the same building, banging on my door at night and going through my garbage in the morning for three months. Then he started depositing large amounts of cash into my bank account. I was in shock. He even put enough cash in there for me to buy a diamond wedding ring I wanted from the store I worked at because we had been legally married for almost two years, and I never had a ring of any kind. He said, "I am working hard, making money, and I even got an apartment in my name here in Atlanta. Now I am coming to get you! Quit your jobs. I am coming to take you back with me, and you don't have to work anymore. My promise has come through." I thought to myself, *My ship has finally come in!* But unfortunately, it had a small hole in the bottom that would eventually sink the entire boat with me in it.

He did come to get me, and Atlanta opened up a new world for me. We lived in a modest apartment for about seven months, piling up cash. But it wasn't long before he wanted more. He said we had to buy a house. I said no we don't. I am comfortable, and I feel safe in life right where we are. He kept pushing me and pushing me, then he even set up a real estate agent to come and pick me up to look at houses he said we could afford. I didn't want to go, but I did. We looked at several houses. I really did like one of the houses and loved another. But like usual, it really didn't matter what I liked or what I wanted. It was all just a scam for him to make me think I was getting to choose. The truth was it was all about him, and he would get exactly what he wanted no matter what he had to do to get it or what lie he had to tell. He brought me himself to this other house that he had wanted, not either of the ones I liked. I had never been shown this house until he brought me there. I did not like it. He pushed me and told me all these things I could do to it and fix it the way I wanted, horse shit and all. And of course, in the end, he was using his credit, not mine because my credit was in the gutter due to a bankruptcy I had four years prior after my divorce. My name was nowhere on the house. How convenient.

I moved on to his plan and did make the expensive changes I wanted to in order to make me feel like it was my home. That's when I started noticing him piling random things that we didn't need or already had plenty of. I had no idea where any of this stuff was coming from. Eventually when I finally counted, there were thirteen computers and laptops both in the house and some in the garage. I asked, "Why do we have all these computers and where did they come from?" He told me he bought two and the rest, customers of his were getting rid of them, so he got them for free or that he had traded services to them to get them. He had grown up dirt poor and was one of six kids with a single mother in Israel, so I thought, *He is just over compensating for what he never had until now.* But the hoarding continued to get worse. Before I knew it, the entire garage was packed to the ceiling and spilling into the house. So I started throwing things away and taking things to the goodwill. Once he noticed, he was furious. We had many blown out arguments over his hoarding habits. I told him, "No matter how much you buy or acquire for free, as you tell me, nothing will ever fill the emptiness of having nothing as a child, and you're a grown man now, let the shit go!" He said okay, but it never stopped. He kept bringing crap back home every day. The truth, I found out later was that he was stealing all these things from unknowing customers houses he was working at. He even brought home thousands of dollars in high-end furniture that he claimed they gave him. It was all bullshit.

I started to become withdrawn because I felt he was not listening to me, nor did he give a damn what I wanted. My mental state started to deteriorate and went downhill fast after that. I started staying in our room most of the time and drinking. The more he stayed out and didn't listen to me, the more I became depressed, angry, and drank more and more. I started hearing the voice of The Monster again loud and clear, saying, "You are not worth anything to him or anyone else in this life." I became very emotionally unstable. So I did what I knew to temporarily feel better, even if for a few moments. I drank. Quickly I became suicidal all over again. I broke down, told him how I was feeling, cried, screamed, threatened to leave him, and begged him not to go out but to stay home with me. I even took a knife from the kitchen and sliced my arms until they were bloody to show him I was dead serious. He looked at me, and for the first time, I saw a glimpse of the man behind the mask. Black eyes that were empty. I told him, "If you walk out that door, when you come home, I promise you I will be dead." The black eyes stared back at me. He said nothing then stepped over on top of me crying on the floor, bloody and went out anyways. Desperate to hang on I called the national suicide prevention hotline; they basically said, "Well, we don't know what to tell you, but you should go on living." I hung up on them and thought to myself, *Live for what?* That was a total waste of time and energy to even pick up the phone and dial. I had enough. Once I sobered up the next day, I packed my shit and left him. But that was not the end by far.

I got an apartment and moved in. I quickly learned that I brought my problems with me. Just because you change the environment around you, it doesn't mean the environment on the inside of you has changed. I tried to move forward with life for about four months. My sister and my son came to visit and stayed with me for the summer. It did bring me joy. But as soon as they left, I was right back to living with emptiness, loneliness, and extreme depression. Suicidal thoughts ran ramped once again. The chosen one started texting and calling and coming by my apartment because he had discovered his life no longer prospered without me. He told me bullshit lies that I wanted to believe so terribly bad. I talked myself into believing it would be different this time. Just like a victim of abuse of any kind wants to truly believe but simply is not true. So I left my apartment and moved back in with him. He promised me the world as usual and even bought a bunch of crap to try to impress me and convince things had changed. I was so mentally and physically exhausted that I decided to just give in and believe him. It only took a year to prove I had made the biggest mistake of my life.

About a month after I had came back, the chosen one told me that we were going to have a baby together, or it was over. All the walls started to cave in on me once again. I wasn't strong enough to fight the devil inside him, so I gave in. As much hurt and pain I had told him about that ate me alive about missing out on being a mother to my son, he promised he would bring back to me no longer mattered to him. Not that it truly ever did in the first place, he only told me what I wanted to hear to ultimately got what he wanted. Never once was it ever about what I wanted or needed. When I became pregnant with our daughter, he talked about how this was my "second chance."

We even went out and bought everything for our baby all on our own, asking or wanting nothing from no one for our new arrival. We painted and decorated and furnished an immaculate nursery that was so beautiful it brought tears to my eyes. And when she arrived two weeks early, we were over the moon with joy and happiness.

Until January 1, 2011, our daughter was two-and-a-half-month old when my world completely fell apart in two seconds. We were in bed that morning, and our baby was sleeping in between us. I on my laptop, he on his. When I got an instant message on my social media page with happy pictures posted of us and our tiny angel that lie in between us in bed that said from a woman, "I just found your husband's social media account page because it is under his legal name I guess, but I know him by his nickname. Here is a link to his dating website profile that says he is not married and has no kids, and I think you should know what a cheating, lying, dirtbag he is because I had been seeing him for almost four months, and I had no idea he had a wife and a newborn baby!" At that very moment, I knew it was the beginning of the end.

I was frozen, just sitting there when I clicked on the link. I then went on autopilot mode as I said to him, "Umm, I got something interesting to show you!" He, of course, said, "What?" I handed my laptop to him, and he read the message and saw the link behind it that I had clicked on. He sat there for a good two minutes with all the blood drained from his face. And what happened next was cold and heartless. He handed it back to me, did not even look at me or our baby daughter, and said, "It will never happen again. Now let's move on." I sat there pondering on it in my mind for a minute. While rage moved up my body and to my face, I got up, put our baby in her room in her crib, I came back, closed the door to our bedroom, and went completely off on him and then broke down crying hysterically. He was unmoved. When I was done, I went to the bathroom and slammed the door, locked it, and stood in the shower crying my eyes out until all the tears were gone and the hot water had turned cold. When I did come out, he had our daughter in his arms, and he said, "Come on, we are going out and go shopping to get you whatever you want." I spoke no words and just got ready like everything was okay. I was a walking zombie the whole day. He wanted to know what I wanted to get. I finally replied, "Nothing, you can't buy what I wanted." So he decided to purchase me a big screen plasma TV for my bedroom since I spend so much time alone in there. We came home and he set it all up for me. I had been talking about getting one for a long time. Now that I had it, I didn't even care.

About a week went by, and he had been on his best behavior and acting like he really gave a damn, but something was not right inside my stomach. I felt an overwhelming feeling of other lies and way more betrayal than I could have ever imagined and a sick, painful knot inside my gut that I could not ignore. But I said nothing to him. When he thought it was safe to start going back out again, he asked if I was okay with him to go out that night back to the pool league he was on. I said, "Yeah, sure." I sat at home with our baby and did the normal. I put her down to sleep eventually, and I came out into the living and drank wine and watched TV. The feeling in my stomach became so intense that I prayed out loud to God to help me. Then suddenly a calmness came over me, and there was a voice inside my head that was not the one I call the monster. It said to me, "He has another secret e-mail account. It is the exact same e-mail address he has now and with the exact same password he uses for everything except it is through a Yahoo account and not a Gmail account." So I instantly went to the one laptop he keeps by the couch on a stand that he checks immediately as soon as he walks through the front door every day like clockwork. I typed in exactly what the voice had told me. I just unlocked the door to hell. I had found where the devil keeps his secrets and where his playground exists. There was two-and-a-half-year worth of disgusting, explicit, pornographic photos and e-mail exchanges between twenty-seven different women. That was only two and a half years, who knows about the entire eight years we had been together. I found the worst picture taken of a five-hundred-pound woman with her legs spread open with her holding all her fat rolls back so you could see her nasty vagina that she could not even see herself, and I made it the screen saver and wallpaper of his laptop.

He never comes home until after midnight when he goes to his pool games. So I did what I never do. I stayed up and in the living room waiting on him to come home. It was 12:40 a.m. when he walked through the door. He said, "What are you doing up?"

I replied, "Nothing, just waiting for you." He said okay and kissed me on the cheek and sat down on the couch and turned on his laptop. As soon as he opened it, he knew. I stood up, took my glass of wine, I said nothing, and walked away to go to bed. He sat there with that image staring back at him. He knew that, at that moment, I had found out the truth about him. He came into the bedroom about ten minutes later and said, "Where is the baby?" I said, "She is in her room." He went to check on her, and she was sleeping. He came in, and all hell broke loose the moment he opened his mouth and tried to give me excuses as to why he had did it. The best reason he gave that sent me way over the edge and to the point of no return was, "Well, it's your fault too because you were sick almost all her pregnancy and didn't want to have sex, so I had to go elsewhere!" I jumped out of that bed and punched him right in the face. I saw nothing but black. He was still talking, but I heard nothing he said after that. I grabbed my 12-gauge shotgun and cocked it back and put it right in his face, and I said, "How would you like to know if Jesus really does exist, you motherfucker?" Looking back now, I wish had pulled the trigger and blew his head right off his shoulders and done my time in prison because I would be out by now, and he would still be dead, but I could go on living my life. But that was not what happened.

Since that night, I have lived in hell. He ran off with my baby girl when our divorce was final. She was six months old. The law allowed him to do so because they said we had joint custody and technically it was not kidnapping at a state or federal level. That was eight and a half years ago. Every time I did find him through the social security number I got him, he moved, and the court system said they "had no jurisdiction." Well, a year ago, I found him again, and I proved jurisdiction through my daughter's school records. But it was still not good enough by a court of law. I have spent, just in legal fees alone in only the last twelve months, $17,000. With little result other than I get a court-ordered phone call with her once a week and a visit with a daughter that doesn't even really know me for two days last year.

I don't care if it costs me a million dollars. I will fight to the end now that I have nailed his ass down and he is in a position currently that he cannot pick and move. The devastation of my sham of a marriage has long been forgotten by me, but what I still die a new death from every single day of my life is knowing that he succeeded in punishing me by removing my daughter from my life because I outed the devil dressed as a holy Jewish man from Israel, and my own country betrayed me by letting him get away with it at every level. I sat and thought all these years and even today, *Maybe he is the chosen one but not by God as he says but by Satan to kill, steal, and destroy everyone and everything around him.* The book of Revelations says it best! "I know of your afflictions and your poverty, yet you are rich! I know about those that claim to be Jews and are not but instead are a Synagogue of Satan" (Revelation 2:9). "I will make those who are of the synagogue of Satan, who claim to be Jews though they are not, but are liars. I will make them come and fall down at your feet and acknowledge that I have loved you" (Revelation 3:9).

Only the word of God has kept me alive until today. I am still waiting and praying to the Lord Jesus and to the Father, God Almighty, that tomorrow will be the day the promise comes true. It is now 2019.

Irony is a pill that once swallowed, leaves you feeling better, but always has a bitter after taste.

—Jennifer Hatton

CHAPTER 6

Emotional Bankruptcy

When you hear the word bankruptcy, you usually think of someone legally finalizing through the court system that they have hit a point in their life to where they can no longer monetarily pay their bills for one reason or another, and that they now are willing to turn over anything of value in order to downsize, to get their finances under and back into control, and to relieve the stress of persistent creditors off their back. In most cases, you are saying that you finally have the humility to humble yourself enough to tell the courts and everyone that knows you that you are no longer able to afford the price you have to pay to sustain the lifestyle you currently have or did have.

Well, I have experienced both a financial bankruptcy and several "emotional bankruptcies." I can honestly tell you that, hands down, the emotional bankruptcy was way harder than losing cash or material items of any kind. The biggest difference for me in a financial bankruptcy and an emotional one is when the day you walk away leaving the courthouse with your judge approved the final discharge papers in hand saying that you are officially and totally broke financially, you feel a sense freedom—a weight lifted from your shoulders. But when you walk away from having a bankruptcy that refers to your emotional state of being, you not only leave with no or little money, credit cards, or material items, but you also walk away with the feeling of extreme loss, trauma, and the emotion of mourning a death. It may be a real, an actual death of a person, or it may be the death of a life you once had. Either way, both are extremely devastating. However, an emotional bankruptcy is something you never forget; something you never get over. Something you carry around inside you that no drug, prescription or illicit, or all the alcohol in the world can ever make you forget. This is the story of my experience of the total loss of everything and everyone I ever had.

When I was growing up as a child until age eighteen, I always said to myself, "Once I get out of this godforsaken place and away from these people, I will go as far away as I can and actually make something of myself unlike the people around me. Those that I was forced to deal with as a child but now no longer have to. Those that have small dreams and little ambition, who I see now live with acceptance of mediocrity and live in denial." Keeping true to my promise, that is exactly what I did! In doing so, I ended up paying a severely high price for the newfound freedom, the big dreams, and endless rainbows I chased. I already knew that I was different from most people—medicated or not. I was still different. Many people questioned my decisions over the years, and most were my own family. Over time, they made me question myself. Every time I stuck my neck out and risked it all to live my dream, then it failed or fell apart. I was *not* personally devastated at that time. I was not happy the day I realized each time it was not going work out, but immediately, my brain was running nonstop on my next idea, thought, and plan. I was fine with failure; I saw and lived it my whole life up until this point, and I never really knew anything different anyways. So why did it really even matter for anyone to put their two cents in? I never said I made the best decisions in life, but I also never thought after my grandmother died when I was nineteen, the total lack of support and encouragement to do better would also die with her. My first mistake was telling anyone in my family what my goals and dreams were because in their eyes, I was labeled crazy long ago. And for some reason, I still saw myself as that little girl just trying to belong somewhere and wanting for someone to be proud of me.

My family made it their personal mission to tell me I was stupid and that I needed to stop long enough to be ashamed of the actions I had done. They made me feel like I had totally lost my mind for not giving up and settling for what I had left and "just be thankful for what little you still got." Some were in shock; some were outraged that I was capable of not being completely defeated and was capable of moving on the very next day. They considered that to be "radical and irrational behavior," because it was not what they knew, understood, or saw themselves growing up. I realize that they meant no true harm in the beginning and were only trying to advise me on what they thought was best; even though I never asked for their opinion. However, by doing so, they planted seeds of doubt and insecurities in my mind that were never there before they opened their mouths. Their harsh words and actions quickly took root inside me and grew leaves of shame that then bloomed flowers of worthlessness and guilt inside myself. It was the same feeling I got when I was growing up, and in my mind, I believed all people were equal in gender, color, and race; they were still people just like me.

I was quickly told by ignorant family members that anyone unlike us should be feared and were not equal to us as human beings. That is the birth of racism. Racism is not a belief or thought that you are born with; it is something you are taught by those you trusted most. Luckily that ignorant belief was not something I held onto, but it was still the same seed that was artificially planted in mind. After a few more times of something not working out for me what I had ventured out to do, my mind started to believe it was true about what they were all saying about me and the decisions I had made. But my heart had a flame inside it that no one could put out. So in trying to be accepted, I finally gave in, and I tried for years after that to be different from what I felt I was truly destined to be—my authentic self. I denied God's orders for me and put it aside to try to conform to being what they called "normal" in today's society. It wasn't long before I became a very angry, hateful, and a resentful person because of it. When all the stress became too much for me to handle and all these different medications and treatments failed, I went looking for something to numb out the pain of living a life I didn't want to live but thought I had too. I quickly found that instant relief in alcohol. So the worse I felt, the more I drank. Then more became all the time, and before I knew it, I was full-blown alcoholic. That is when

I started writing checks out of my emotional bank account that was already overdrawn.

Then one by one, they just kept bouncing. I drank heavily in order to suppress my feelings of guilt, shame, and not being good enough by the standards of others around me. It also quieted the voice of the one I call The Monster. I started acting out again like I did when I was a child trapped in something I did not wanna be in. But everyone else seemed to be as happy as a bee, that I was highly medicated with psychiatric drugs and living the life they thought I should, but inside I was slowly disappearing again, quietly fading away. I didn't have a basement to run to anymore, so instead I ran to dimly lit bars. A very dangerous thing started to take shape with in me. The real, true person I had been hiding inside me in order to please others was growing stronger and more powerful until one day, it overpowered the fake me.

The day finally came when the authentic me outgrew the body I lived in. She now had took on a life of her own. I was very angry at myself and at others for convincing me for decades that I had to be this other person, and that society and my family would not accept me unless I did. And *yes*, I am well aware that I acted out against people even those that were innocent due to the extreme anger I had built up inside me. What puzzles me the most is if someone constantly screams, hits, torments, or abuses a dog for a period of time, eventually one day that dog has had enough and finally snaps and fights back and bites or attacks them, leaving them bloody and traumatized; and they actually wonder why that happened? They have the nerve to blame the dog and have him put down. Shouldn't it be the abuser of the animal that gets the death penalty and not the dog? Do you really need a PhD to understand that one?

I also admit that I wanted everyone to pay for what others had done to me guilty or not. I can now tell you at that particular time in my life that I opened the door to the devil dressed as an angel, and that I knew exactly who he was and he did not fool me this time unlike the chosen one. I was so brazen at that time I thought to myself, *I am going to invite this devil in disguise into my home since he thinks he has me fooled, and I am gonna take him on all by myself.*

So I did. I invited him in and had him sit at my dinner table and tell me bullshit lies, like the ones The Monster had been telling me my whole life. But this time, I thought, *It would be different because I had the upper hand now, the knowledge, and the homecourt advantage.* That turned out to be a very stupid decision on my part in the end. I quickly learned that I was no match for Satan in disguise and that only God could and would be able to remove him from my life and my home that he now dwelled in. It took me years and thousands of prayers to God to get him out. I guess the worst thing of all about my bad decision to try to take on the devil wasn't himself or the havoc he reeked; it was all of my so-called friends and family that no longer stood by my side, and I stood all alone, just me, the devil, my disease, and a full bottle of tequila.

In the summer of 2011, that today still haunts and hurts me to the core, I have confronted all those involved more than once, and still, *no one* will give me a simple apology; they would rather see me dead than to say they were sorry. I know because I threatened suicide and, in some cases, did attempt to take my own life, yet nothing changed them. They were unmoved. In May of 2011, the court had finalized my divorce, assets, and my six-month-old baby girl. The court gave me nothing; they gave me my own personal items that I only brought into the marriage, $1,267 in cash, a broken down van with no back seats and filled with fumes of carpet cleaning chemicals once used in our business, and my dog named Louie. That was it. Everything else, including my $250K home, my $40K Jaguar, all the belongings inside the house that we both bought together, the extensive amount of cash in our joint bank account that my ex-husband took out immediately after he knew I was filing for divorce, and most importantly my tiny baby girl, was all awarded to him.

At that time, I felt defeat and devastation like never before. All was given to a man that was a proven criminal, cheater, and a pitiful excuse of human life. The truly puzzling thought to me was, Why? I had done nothing wrong in the eyes of the law. I was not a criminal. I was not a drug addict. Nor was I even a bad person. But two different judges in two different states both said my baby daughter would be better off with a man that was not even a legal US citizen. How does that happen you say? The only thing my multiple attorneys could give me as an excuse or reason why was this, and I quote, "Jennifer, in the eyes of the law today, they consider any diagnosis of any kind of mental illness as a chronic disease. That cannot be truly monitored by the court that you will continuously take your meds as prescribed and see your psychiatrist regularly, as well your therapist. The court just doesn't have the funding to keep up on that. Therefore, they would rather give custody to a parent that does not have a documented diagnosis of any mental issues."

I said, "My diagnoses are not schizophrenia, narcissism, or multiple personalities. They are in fact; A-Typical depression, severe anxiety, post-traumatic stress disorder, and unipolar disorder." "But, Jennifer, at this stage in the world and in the legal system, all mental illness diagnoses are considered the same." I replied, "So what you are saying is that if I was convicted for any level of an assault charge, that I can spend as much time in jail, as someone convicted of murder?" The response was, "Unfortunately yes, maybe in thirty or forty years, the court will adopt a different law or reasoning, but today that is just how it is."

From that point, I tried to pick up the broken and missing pieces of my life and started to attempt to glue them back together somehow. I was angry. I was emotionally and mentally beaten down. And my drinking continued to soar to new heights and new levels. However, I knew I needed someone, even a group of people to lean on for love and support at this point. The normal thought of most people would be to turn to your blood relatives. Oh, how wrong I was! I was invited to a family cookout of some sort that started at my sister and her boyfriend's house that is now her husband as well as I was spending my last week with my baby daughter before my ex took her over and moved to another state, not knowing when or if I would see her again. My ten-year-old son was going to be there as well since he lived with his father just down the street. So of course, I wanted to go and be around people I thought loved and supported me through this horrific time in my life. I came with my baby girl, my boyfriend that I reconnected with from high school, and his seven-year-old daughter. Everything was fine when we arrived, and they had asked us to bring extra ice. I was ready for a fun and relaxing time with loved ones and my two children together for maybe the last time since the future was uncertain about me and both of them.

We were there about an hour and a half when they were finally ready with the food to move the gathering to just walking distance down to my ex-husband's and his wife's house where they have a community pool. They packed up all the food and drinks and said absolutely nothing to me while doing so. Then my mother stepped in front of me and said, "Umm, where do you think you guys are going?"

I said, "Huh…what do you mean?" Then she quietly pulled me aside, leaving my boyfriend and his daughter alone in the living room and said to me, "Oh, I thought you knew you were not invited to the food and pool party." I said, "What the hell are you talking about?" She then said, "Well I assumed you understood that since you started an argument with your son's stepmother the other week about something you did not agree with her about." I replied, "You mean, when I stood up to her and set her straight about the hateful lies she was telling my son about me, my life, and who I choose to be in a relationship with that is not her business or place to tell him that?" She said, "Well, you just can't act like that and expect people to want to invite you for family-friendly gatherings, but both of your children are going." Flames came from the pit of my stomach into my chest, then through my neck, and into my head and face. I then lost it completely. I admit that I then did the following: I cursed and screamed at my birth mother, calling her every name in the book and even getting up in her face as though I was gonna hit or slap her for choosing the side of water instead of blood, despite what she knew I had been going through for the last seven months. And I promise you that it was God or the Holy Spirit that stepped in between us and pulled me back from physically assaulting her. Because trust me, the level of anger and betrayal I felt right at that moment was so extreme that I did not care what it would have cost me to hit her. I had already lost everything and was at the lowest point of my life then anyways. I was so shocked that my own mother and sister did not do the right thing and take up for me. Instead, they chose to be weak and "not rock the boat" and place a knife in my back instead, right after I had just recently completed pulling out all the knives that my daughter's father had placed in my face!

When someone stabs you in the back, they do it because they are too scared to stab you in the front, and they just hope since you didn't see them doing it, that you will never know who exactly who did it. Only someone of pure evil and the heart of the devil has the guts to stab you in the face or the front so that you can see it coming and that you know exactly who it is that did it. At that point, I left without my children, just myself and my boyfriend and his daughter. I said nothing to them even though he grilled me in the car. The anger and humiliation was too much for me to get the words out. I dropped them off and went straight to the bar where I drowned my pain in enough alcohol to kill a 250lb man. I called a cab home and left my car at the bar. Soon after, my boyfriend broke up with me. Not surprising.

My downward spiral continued from there with dating and even marrying a total loser of a man all because I thought that was all I deserved at that point, and every bottom feeder man I was with, of course, never had a job, a car, a driver's license, any money, and no place to live. So I paid for their total, complete personal existence while they were with me. But I was determined that no matter what, I was gonna make it all on my own, regardless of the price I had to pay to do so. I had a professional job, but it was not a high-paying career like a doctor or lawyer. Even with my major cut in expenses and no credit cards anymore, I could not make ends meet.

I got myself a small house in a very nice and clean neighborhood. And even took in many different roommates to try to pay the bills. *None* of them ever had intentions of paying me, so I ended up paying my personal bills and their living expenses myself, including household bills, their food, their booze, and their cigarettes. To make ends meet, I even swallowed my pride and dignity, as if I had any really left anyways, and started becoming a high-dollar prostitute. Not the kind that walks the streets but one that uses wealthy acquaintances and the Internet to lure men with lots of cash that wanted more than what they got at home. The funny thing is that both my mother and my sister knew what I was doing because I told them to their face and over the phone as well as the multiple room-mates I took in knew exactly what I had to do to pay my bills and theirs too, and *no one* gave a damn as to what I had to do to make ends meet. No one offered to help me. No one offered to sign for me a credit card to balance things out so I could make payments on it myself and in order not to do what I had to do to keep the lights on, the rent paid, and afford food. *Not a damn one*!

That is fucking pitiful on everyone's part that knew and could have done something, but all had the same lame ass excuse as to why they could not help me. I sold my soul to the devil, and it took me five years to pay him enough to get it back. That is a type bankruptcy that you never forget. The one you never get over.

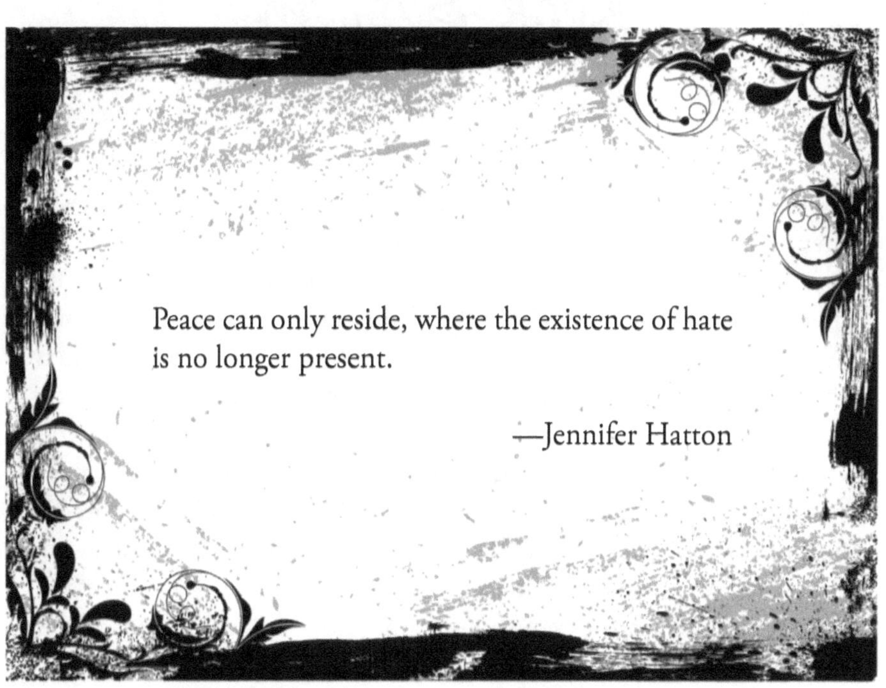

Peace can only reside, where the existence of hate
is no longer present.

—Jennifer Hatton

CHAPTER 7

Rock Bottom

Most people go through life, thinking every hard time or tragedy they've already experienced, is the worst thing that could possibly ever happen to them. When they reach what they consider to be their lowest point, they believe they have hit the very bottom of life. What they don't know or realize yet is if a bottom still exists to catch their fall, they then still have much further to go in order to reach the point where the bottom actually falls out. The reality is you will continue to drop lower and deeper into the pit until the day comes when you find yourself all alone in total darkness, silence, and no one any longer gives a damn, like you never existed. No one answers your calls, responds to your texts, and no one comes to open the door when you knock even though you know they are home. When that time comes, you find yourself falling to your knees begging and praying to a God that you're not even sure really exists. You really do not know how bad it truly is until it continues to get worse and there is no bottom in sight. That is what I define as rock bottom. It is a black hole you fall into backward, almost as if you were pushed off a cliff, but the hole has no light, just complete darkness with no sounds besides your own. You can feel the breeze on your back, your arms and legs in the wind as you fall backward, and your trying to grasp something, anything to hold on to, but nothing is there. You have total fear and severe panic and extreme anxiety in your heart and mind of not knowing when or if you will ever reach the end.

Only then do you appreciate the problems, hard times, and tragedies of the past you only thought you had.

There are really no words to describe the feeling or emotion of having no one to turn to and that no one cares. Today I personally question if there is a place called hell that bad people go to after they die, as "heavens rejects," to spend eternity in pain, torture, and condemnation as a punishment for who they were as a person or what they did when they were alive. But I can tell you that hell is a real place that exists right here on earth, and I lived there for years, and some days, I still go back to visit, always against my will. Hell is much like an RV on wheels. It moves around, and sometimes decides to stop and set up camp right inside your very own mind. It is where The Monster lives, dwells, and sleeps. I try to be quiet and not to wake him, much like I did as a child with my grandfather when I played with my toys in the basement. I try to drug my mind on a daily basis with psychiatric meds and alcohol to keep him sleeping, but eventually, he does wake up. And the havoc and chaos he causes inside me unleashes a domino effect that makes me lash out in different forms but always in hurtful ways to myself as well as anyone around me.

I hurt myself by cutting my arms with knives or razor blades in order to feel a sense of peace or control that I felt I had lost. Then I stop once I feel I have regained the power over myself back. I hurt others by hateful words, actions, or physical violence against them. I am always regretful of what I have done once The Monster leaves. By then, it's too late to take back, too late to fix the internal and external scars I caused to myself and others. So I clean up and bandage my self-inflicted wounds and try to repair what I have done around me. But most people don't care to hear my apologies, nor do they believe or want to hear about the one I call The Monster. They believe I am making it all up or using it as an excuse for the actions I have taken because they don't see him physically nor does he dwell inside their minds. The ironic thing is they don't believe in what they cannot see, hear, feel, or touch, but they do believe in an existence of a God they have also never seen, heard, or touched. Only those plagued by mental illness understand and know exactly who he is and what he is truly capable of. And that you often believe the power he has over you is greater than the God you pray to.

I always thought growing up, that no matter what happens in this life, at the very least, I would always have my family to fall back on to support me through whatever happened. I always heard and saw on TV and in the church, that your family is all you have to count on in the end. Maybe that is a true statement for some, but it's definitely not true for me or for millions of other people all over the world I have learned over the years. Irony is a pill that once swallowed, leaves a very bitter and long after taste. The irony, in this case, is if a member of my family came to my door and knocked on it, I would open it and let them in regardless of how they turned their backs on me in the past or the scars I still have from the knives they stabbed me in the back with. Even though I know for a fact they would not do the same for me in return. People say, "Let them go. Who cares? Move on." My question is, "Move on to what?"

My foundation has completely crumbled and fell apart. My pain still feels like it happened just yesterday. How can I possibly close a book if the chapters are still being written? I still wonder what I had done that was so horrific that I was branded unforgivable and now I am considered an outcast. I am no longer invited or welcomed at family functions, birthday celebrations, Thanksgiving, or even Christmas. The only thing I am guilty of is speaking the truth of what was really going on inside me, my mind, and my life. And I did tell the raw truth of what I saw going on with those around me.

I understand people don't like it when you put a mirror right in front of their face so they can see what is actually staring right back at them. I didn't either when mental hospitals, jail, and the court system did it to me, but that was the only way I could make the changes needed inside myself and the dysfunctional life I was living. Isn't that what everyone really wants? To be capable of making the changes necessary to live a better life tomorrow than what they lived today? Or do they just want everyone to listen to their problems but do nothing about it? Change can only happen if you are willing to accept and acknowledge what the reality is and then take ownership of it. But for me, I have been given the *death penalty* as a sentence for the so-called crimes I committed against people and myself where that particular punishment was not even on the table.

I never realized that in the court of public opinion, I am deemed unforgivable, worthless, and a lost cause. The thing I find the most interesting is that I watch true crime stories all the time, and I see people who truly did brutally murder their entire immediate family inside their own homes, including their spouse, their children, and even their family dog. Then I watch them go to trial and be convicted. Then on sentencing day, they are standing alone at the podium and sitting right behind them on benches in the court room is the rest of their surviving family members just waiting for their opportunity to plea to the judge or jury not to give them death penalty but life in prison. I ask, "How does that work?" I haven't done anything like that or even remotely close, and I can't even get a phone call or a text back from those that claimed they once loved me for decades but longer. Wherever I stand in life, I turn around and I look behind me, and I see no one staring back at me. That right there is enough to make me a full-blown alcoholic. I don't even need to roll in the mental illness factor. This is the true story of me hitting rock bottom.

When you break someone's spirit, much like breaking a wild horse, you get the same result—both the horse and the person can never go back to what they used to be no matter how much time passes. After my second marriage had failed, I fell lower and lower into a dark pit with no bottom. I guess my expectations of those I thought loved me was greatly overestimated in my mind and in my heart. The sad thing is that I truly believed my family would step up 100 percent and back me up and support me to get back on my feet again. I obviously was very wrong, and because of it, I was so outraged and devastated that I said, "You know what, *fuck it* and everyone around me with your bullshit, empty promises, and lies!" I lost all control of the tiny piece of the pie that was me that still existed. I then let The Monster take total control because I could no longer cope with now having basically no one to help me pick up the broken pieces of my life and put me back together again. From that very point, it was a downward spiral that took me to a new low, that I had never reached before.

My mother and stepfather did come down from Kentucky to get me, and they did loan me money on a credit card to pay for a lawyer that got me nothing and nowhere. My ex had gotten a "cease and desist order" then had me physically removed from my own home by a sheriff. My mother and stepfather left me there and went back home to Kentucky. I came on my own back to Kentucky about two months later. Once my next-door neighbor started having serious issues with his wife and kids, I had been staying with them since I had nowhere else to go once the sheriff had escorted me out of my house by ex-husband's court order.

The plan was that my twenty-year-old sister and her "boy-friend" of a year were going to let me stay in their new two-bedroom apartment back home in exchange for either four hundred dollars a month in cash or the four hundred dollars a month I now got in food stamps which that arrangement lasted less than a month. Her then boyfriend who was ten years younger than me and about twenty years younger in life experience and maturity had come home from work briefly while I was looking online and applying for jobs. I was extremely devastated but was trying to move forward with what little life I had left and at the same time I was preparing to cook dinner for them later with the food I just bought with government money assistance I was now forced to asked for. I had it had it all laid out when he came from a job I *got him* through a friend of mine since he had no training, no skills, no college degree, no experience in really anything and were struggling to make ends meet well before I moved there. I called my friend to help out my sister because I loved her and heard the stress and tears over the phone about how her check barely covered the rent while he had no job. I helped them get stable and open a door for him that was not possible before me, doing HVAC work. He had no way in hell of getting into that line of work without me and my friend who had thirty years and a master's license in HVAC work. And that ungrateful bastard had the nerve to come home when I was drinking a glass of wine and applying for jobs and trying to hold myself together at the same time and said to me, "Wow look, it's two thirty in the afternoon, and you're drinking already. What a shock!" Who does that? I lost it right there. I said, and I quote, "Who in the hell do you think you are? I am not drunk or taking shots. I am having some wine to calm my nerves while applying for my seventh job today which is about seven times more jobs than what you had applied for in two months before I even got here. I just lost everything including my second baby, and I do you a favor and get you a job, a supply four-hundred-dollars-worth of food in your apartment when you had nothing but canned soup and a bunch of seasonings. How dare you open your damn mouth and say something like that to me!" Of course, he had no reply because it was all true. He just stormed out and slammed the door. Then like fifteen minutes later, my sister comes home, crying and screaming at me for making her boyfriend upset and that he wants me out now. I told her everything he said and reminded her of what I did for her with getting him a job and the food I brought into the house that was just dust in the cabinets before.

She didn't care and, at that moment, was when she chose a stupid boy/man of a year together over me, and that was the first time she ever stabbed me in the back per se all because she didn't want to be alone and was not strong enough to make it on her own. I, of course, said "Fuck it and fuck both of you." I grabbed a few things and walked out. Two days later, she texted me to come get the rest of my stuff when I had nowhere to go. I called my mother, and she took my sister and her boyfriend's side over mine even though I told her the 100 percent truth, and I was not wrong in this situation.

She did not care, and at that moment, I realized a second knife was now in my back. How could anyone possibly find that behavior okay? I ask; especially if you personally witnessed what my ex-husband just had done to me? Not even thanking me for the job I got for her boyfriend who is now her husband and father of her one small son and another now on the way. I relieved an enormous amount of stress off my sister, but I guess that wasn't enough or even that she remembered at that point. All she was thinking in her mind, I believe was, *I can't lose another man/boy because the only real relationship I had before him turned out that he was gay and my plans of a family and marriage he proposed were destroyed and shattered by the truth that I didn't want to see, much like my mother who married the first man who came along, had a child with him (which was my older sister) and my mother and I both chose to ignore all the signs and red flags we both saw along the way, but we both were just too weak and ignorant to stand on our own.*

In my mind, it brought back my memories of being a small child that my mother thought of me as the baggage left over from a teenage failed marriage. She maybe never said those words, but that was how she made me feel. There was absolutely no other reason possible with the proof and evidence I had along with my true side of the story as well as the fact that I was now thirty-two years old and my naive sister was only twenty-two. That my mother could possibly take my sister's side because she saw herself in my sister at that moment—"her innocent angel child of privilege" and her stupid, arrogant boyfriend and believed and sided totally with them and ignored completely what I was saying. I came to get my things and return her key and her boyfriend had put what little things I did have left and my baby daughter's clothes, diapers, and toys and put them in pile not even nice or neat, but a pile-like trash in the living room. I used garbage bags to haul it all out. And moved my "trash," also called my belongings, to my dad's apartment to a mattress on the floor when I already knew my dad was not feeling well in his mind and was ready to explode at any time with his multiple mental illness diagnoses. I didn't bother even saying a word to them about what I now was about to walk into; because their words and actions showed me that, they didn't care anyways. I fell deeper into the black hole.

Soon after, I lowered my standards in my life and what I was willing to accept versus who I really was and deserved and took the next man that showed any interest in me, so I was accepted by someone, by anyone. Since I had now lost even the support of a family, I thought I had and could count on the most devastating and unjust point in life. My drinking continued to increase to a whole new level so that I could numb out my pain, devastation, and the betrayal of everyone, including the sound of the voice of The Monster himself, that I now heard louder than ever. My father had introduced me to a man a few years younger than me, that I wasn't even attracted too, but showed unbelievable interest in me. He worked as a dishwasher/ cook and busboy at a restaurant my dad had met when he worked there part-time to make ends meet since social security mental disability wasn't enough for anyone to live on and survive alone in these times. I married that man that turned out to be a petty thief, liar, alcoholic, and a crackhead who had seventeen pages of criminal history that I was given to by the state when I had to go to court to get a restraining order against him to leave me alone because I got tired of his extreme alcohol and drug use that kept him up all night every night.

It had gotten so bad to the point I could not sleep at night ever because he would come into my room in the middle of the night, yelling and screaming at me, getting in my face, stealing any and all money, prescription medications, jewelry I had, my car, and anything of value that was in my house to pay for his crack habit and cheap alcohol. I stayed for as long as I did with him because I loved his mother way more than him. She was everything I had *ever* wanted in a mother. She was loving, understanding, and accepting of me as her own daughter regardless of my faults, baggage, and mental and emotional issues. She was *always* willing to help me in anyway with anything I needed; regardless if it put her own self out. She helped me when I struggled with money; since I always had a full-time job but still could not make ends meet every month. She signed for anything I needed, not wanted, but needed without bitching, complaining, or making me feel like "a stupid piece of shit because I was unable to do it all on my own."

Unlike my own mother, when I asked to borrow money or credit, she would not freely give it to me, but put me through a lecture, made me feel totally retarded, and then acted like I was asking her to mortgage her own house that she has owned out right for the last twelve years or so. Not to mention how I had to listen to her bitch, complain, and tell me every single damn time I asked. She would say, "You need to learn to get it together, and I can't keep loaning you money or let you use my personal credit cards for your problems." Even though in the end, I paid her back and/or she stole it back from what little inheritance my grandfather had left me. I guess thirty some thousand dollars she got wasn't enough. She made me feel like I was the lowest piece of shit that ever walked this earth. What my own mother never knew was that I always wrote down what I had borrowed, and I made many deposits back into her bank account or I handed her or my sister cash. But conveniently, she doesn't remember that, nor did she remember in 2012 when I got a tax refund of $4,500, I gave it *all* to my sister, had her count it all out at her kitchen table, and deposit it into an account I was told that her and my sister shared together at that point. Hmm, that raised a red flag to me—my mother and sister shared a bank account together, but I left that one alone. In total, I had borrowed about twenty thousand dollars, which I used to pay lawyer fee's for my divorce and attempts to get my baby back (which never happened, and the battle is still ongoing today; she is now almost nine years old).

I no longer have anything to do with my mother. It's simply a painful battle that can never be won. My ex mother-in-law, however, I still wish today that I still had a relationship with. Even though I divorced her son, that now sits in prison for Grand-Theft. She loved and accepted my two kids as her own true grandchildren, buying and supplying them anything they wanted or needed that I could not provide. They even called her "nana." I felt so defeated and destroyed once again after I figured out the real and whole truth about her son. I still stayed married to him for another four years and tried to hide the truth about him from others, but it was kinda hard to hide when your husband spends months in jail or a year in prison. Because even though I knew his mother loved me and my kids as her own, unfortunately, blood is thicker than water; and I knew if I divorced him, I would be divorcing her as well.

She was and still today is a great woman, but even though she knew exactly who her son was and admitted it, she still, in her heart and mind, could not and would not turn her back on him regardless of whatever crime he committed, or how many years he spent incarcerated. She felt like she would be betraying him if she still kept me as her daughter and kept a relationship with my kids as her own grandchildren. That was one of the hardest decisions and heartbreaks

I had felt, to lose the mother I thought God had given me to replace the one I never really had, and then willingly, I had to make the choice to end it all because I couldn't stay married to a disaster of a man that no one could save or change. I died inside once again.

Hurting people, hurt other people.

—Joyce Meyer

CHAPTER 8

Irretrievably Broken

The term, "irretrievably broken" is most commonly used in legal matters concerning divorce. One definition of irretrievable is: "Impossible to correct or return to a previously existing situation or condition." Broken has been defined as: "Having been fractured or damaged and no longer in one piece or working order." If the two meanings of the phrase are put together, then you have exactly the definition of how I feel about my life.

I feel as though I am forever and permanently shattered into a thousand pieces, and it is now impossible for me to ever return to my previous condition of once having hope and faith due to the fact that so many of my pieces have been lost. It's as though you are trying to put together a 1500-piece puzzle, and you get almost to the very end, then you figure out there are still twenty-five holes, and you only have five pieces left. Then you become angry that you wasted all this time putting something together that never can be complete. I have spent so many years trying to put my life all back together, only to find out that I will never be 100 percent whole. At the very best, I can be 85 percent. They teach you, in recovery of any kind, may it be mental, physical, emotional, or substance related, that half the battle is knowing, accepting, and acknowledging to yourself and to others that you have a problem and are now ready to accept help in order to get back on the right path. What they don't teach you is that once you are on the path, do the work, make it through all the steps, and become what they call "a new person," you still will have missing pieces and empty holes with nothing to fill it with. But I guess if they advertised the whole truth, then no one would even try to get better.

Imagine if you had one or both legs amputated, the professionals tell you, "In time with the proper treatment and extensive work on your behalf, you will walk again." So you get past the surgeries, the pain, the grueling physical rehab process, come to terms with the devastation of looking down and seeing a different body than the one you had is no more, then your fitted with prosthetic legs, and yes, you can physically walk again. However, no matter what you do or how much you pray, you will never have your real legs back again, and you will be reminded of what you had lost every single day of your life until you die by having to take off and put on your plastic legs you now have. I understand they are only trying to give you the very best back that you could ever possibly have, but it doesn't change how you feel on the inside. The common misconception with the world is if you change the outside of someone or the outside circumstances, you also change the inside of them as well. Unfortunately, it does not work like that, and the continuous belief of that is totally stupid. The outside can never really change until the inside is changed first.

I ask God why I will never be good enough to have the possible life that was stolen from me? I say, "God, why is it that I have lived through hell and then made bad choices based on the hell I survived and fought back to redeem myself, and no matter how hard or long I work at it, I will never be complete or change all the minds of others about me?" He remains silent even today. I will never get back those years I lost with my children. I will never get back the ones I loved that passed away. And I will never be able to forget the scars I still feel from all the knives in my back. The disappointments, the broken hearts, and the plain devastation of this life as a person with mental illness; that haunts me where ever I go. If I could take back all the pain I caused people with my illness over four decades, I would. But no one ever has said they would do the same for me. I am tired and exhausted from trying to prove myself to everyone. I am tired of trying to convince people that I am not crazy and that I am just like them, only human. Many times a day I think to myself, *Where do I belong? Where is the family I can be a part of?* The reality is that I belong nowhere, and there is no family looking or waiting for me, and that I am a forty-year-old orphan that no one wants to adopt.

I try to reach out to those I still love, and they hang up on me, close the door in my face, and don't respond to the messages I send them. It makes me feel like what The Monster told me is true—I am trash, I am not worthy of human affection, I don't deserve happiness, I don't belong anywhere, and I am a waste of human life. I often pray to God to kill me so that I won't have to do it myself. The greatest fear that have is if I do try to commit suicide, like everything else in my life, it will go wrong, and I won't die. I will survive but be severely disabled and trapped inside my mind with only me and The Monster. I will not be able to move, speak, or even see, just me and him trapped in the same small space for the next forty years or so till my body finally gives out.

I keep hoping and praying for a miracle that most likely will never come. I don't even bother anymore trying to explain my life, my pain, or the horror of what I have seen that still exists when I close my eyes. Most people don't understand, nor can they wrap their heads around my reality. If I told my therapists or psychiatrists what was really going on in my mind, they would have a legal obligation to lock me up because "man's law" is so effective as we all know. What a joke! Let's take someone that is already so damaged and wants to die and let's put them with a bunch of other people who feel the same way and lock them up together until they can't take it anymore and will lie and tell us what we want to hear: "I am all better now. I no longer want to die." Then legally we can discharge them even though they really are still locked up inside their own minds and will never truly be free, destined to be back here in the same mental hospital for the exact same reason soon or, even worse, dead.

I don't bother talking about what is really going on inside me to the few loved ones I still have contact with or the couple of friends I trust because it, too, is not effective. All they do is look at me with a blank stare and say, "Well maybe, it will get better or easier over time." Then they run like hell or act like I never said anything at all and continue on with their lives. I know it is not their fault. I know these few people do love me, but they just can't grasp in their own minds about what I am saying to them, so they are scared they might say or do the wrong thing. So instead, they say or do basically nothing, and it was all just a waste of time for the both of us. So now, I keep my mouth shut to the human world and speak directly only to God, and I write the truth on paper so that maybe someday, someone will read it and might be able to identify with it and not feel as alone as I do today.

I still find myself still looking for reasoning, trying to figure out why I am the way I am. Why I made the choices I did, and when did I become no longer a child that needed to be protected but wasn't to now being an adult that is still neglected and abused by the ones that said they loved me most at one time? What crime or offense did I commit that deserved the punishment I got? Some days I can make it through, others I plan my death—my freedom from a life not worth the pain anymore.

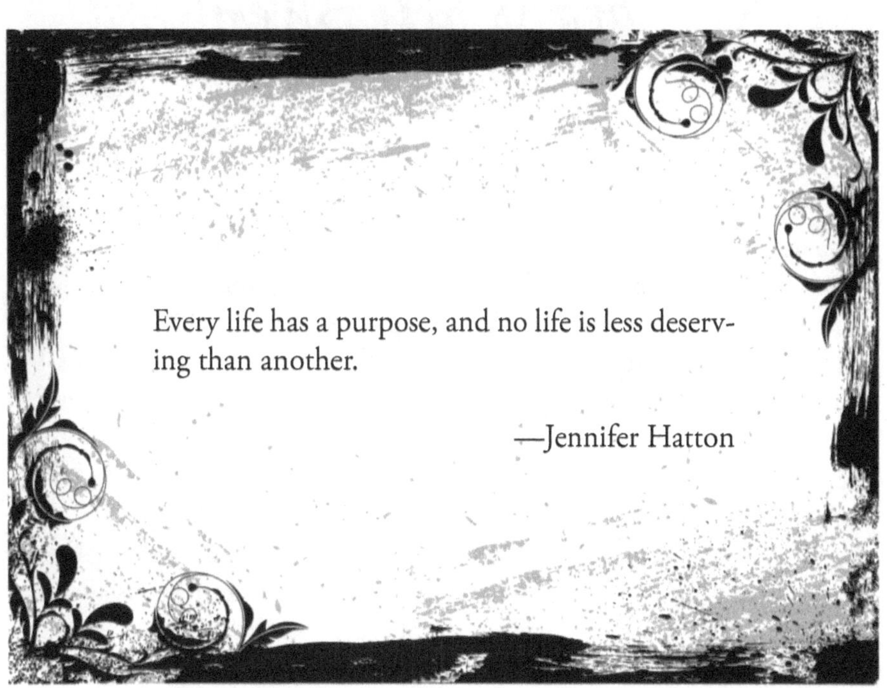
Every life has a purpose, and no life is less deserving than another.

—Jennifer Hatton

CHAPTER 9

The Lord Is My Shepherd

A Psalm of David, "The Lord is my shepherd, I shall not want. He makes me lie down in green pastures, he leads me beside still waters, he restores my soul: he leads me in the paths of righteousness for his name's sake. Yea though I walk through the valley of the shadow of death, I will fear no evil: for you are with me; thy rod and thy staff they comfort me. You prepare a table before me in the presence of my enemies: you anoint my head with oil; my cup runneth over. Surely goodness and mercy shall follow me all the days of my life: and I will dwell in the house of the Lord forever" (Psalm 23:1–6).

I have found that through everything I have done, battles I have fought and lost, dreams that have been shattered, and hearts that I have broken that first broke me, I realized I did it all out of the pain I suffered mentally, emotionally, verbally, and sometimes, physically. And I thought that it was my responsibility to punish those around me, to seek revenge and justice that I truly did deserve but never saw. It did not matter to me whether they contributed to my devastation or not. I wanted someone, anyone to pay for crimes done against me. And by doing so, I lost all connection with the outside world as I knew it to be. I have had to start over and over so many times that I lost count decades ago. A wise woman says it best by this quote, "Hurting people hurt other people." Today I walk alone in what is left of my journey. Yes, I have my beloved James, my father, and my last living uncle, but they haven't seen what I have seen. They have not felt the total betrayal and bore the scars of hundreds of knife wounds in my back. Besides my father, they know not of The Monster that dwells inside my mind that I go to battle with everyday of my life.

None of them have never stared in to the eyes of the devil and then dared to take him on. And because they have not experienced this personally, they are not willing to go to the extremes that I would and that I have, nor do they have the strength and the courage to simply walk away from it all; just as I have already done. Although I love them and would give anything to help them, even kill for them, they cannot honestly say they would do the same for me. At first, that made me very angry inside that the only ones I have left that I love could not or would not go to the ultimate sacrifices I have already made in this life and would make for them in a second. I had several alcohol-driven arguments as well as many sober arguments with each of them as to why they would not do the same for me. None of them could ever give me a true and justifiable answer to that question that was ever good enough for me to understand or accept. However today, I no longer care to fight that battle with them. But in my heart, my willingness to go as far as I need to in order to help them, save them, or defend them still stands today and always will. Much like a mountain that cannot ever be moved, my mind can never change on that.

So when I say to you that I walk alone, I do walk without any human next to me; but instead, I walk with those that have good intensions and love for me but are "Peters" in disguise. Those humans that say I would go to the ends of the earth for you, but in the end, just like Jesus, deny me in the hour I needed the most. I have found that only God is always beside me and never denies me or forsakes me. A God that will and has done any and everything to keep me going, interrupted my suicide attempts right when I had my weapon in my hand, gives me hope and strength, and bring justice to those that murdered me spiritually and emotionally. Because Lord knows I have never and will never see that justice done here on this earth. He is truly the only one that has and never will let me down; he is the only being that can be fully trusted in all things.

At my lowest point, sitting in my jail cell on a cold concrete floor with a Velcro-type straitjacket and no clothes because I was on suicide watch, he was there. He heard my cries when the guards did not care and no one came to see me two out of the three times I was put in there. Or the two times I checked myself into a mental hospital for what I call "a total nervous breakdown," and again, no one came. But he was there. My question to today's society is, "Are you really willing to go as far as it takes to save or rescue someone that you claim to love?" Well, I pray for you that you never really find out the true answer because the reality is that you got a 99 percent chance that they won't. Only God is there in the beginning, and only God will be there in the end.

Dr. Phil says, "Do you want to be right, or do you want to be happy"? Well, my response to that is both. I have learned that I cannot be happy living a lie. Maybe some people can but not me. I have tried for decades now to hold my tongue, pretend things aren't happening, and to live a life that makes everyone around me accept and want me in their "fake ass, fairy tale dream world that simply does not exist." When I did conform to this "plastic-type" lifestyle, all it did was bottle up inside me the hurt, the anger, and the rage I felt by not being my authentic self, never being good enough by human life standards. The best way to kill something or someone, is to simply stop feeding it. If it is not fed, it will not sustain life or will not ever grow larger than what it already is. But me living in denial in order to not rock the boat, gave life to and fed the one I call The Monster. Then he grew in my mind and very soon became stronger and way more powerful than I could handle. There is only so much steam you can bottle up inside anything until it blows or explodes. That is exactly what happened to me. I put on a mask that everyone wanted to see me wear and in order for me to cope with being and living as someone I was not. I found chemicals that could numb out or make me not give a damn anymore. I used massive amounts of prescribed psychiatric drugs as well as alcohol to conform to being this other person. The Monster loved it because he knew then he had taken all control of my mind because now I was totally chemically dependent and did not have the strength to fight him off any longer. I learned then that I would rather die than live in a house of lies. It wasn't till I finally exploded and lost everything I had and pretty much everyone I once believed would always be there that I then started to hear the voice of the Lord in the background of The Monster. The more I listened to God, the less I could hear the lies the other one was telling me. The Lord began to rebuild me; he told I was something: I was special and that he had bigger plans for me than the life I had lost. I felt devastation and hope at the same time. He said I didn't have to change myself in order to follow him, but if I followed him, I would change.

This new and unknown territory was extremely scary to me at first. But when I saw the impact and difference of outcomes it made by listening and doing what he said, I finally felt a peace come over me and a power I never knew existed. He said, "Forget what you thought of as your family, your so-called friends, and the life you had before. I will provide you with a new one. One that is true. One that will accept you and never give up on you, but only if you do as I say."

Psalm 27:10 spoke to my heart saying, "Though my father and my mother forsake me, the Lord will receive me as his own." God also told me that if I stepped off the road he had paved for me, then everything he was doing for me would stop until I got back on the road exactly where I had left off. And I know for sure that was and is still true today. I am not God. I am not Jesus, for I am human. And yes, there are days, weeks, and months where I get distracted, lose focus, and I step off his road; and just like his promise, I become a hamster on a wheel. I am going really fast but going absolutely nowhere! When I choose to get back on his path, he is there waiting for me exactly at the place I stepped off. And that right there is enough to bring me to my knees every time, crying and kneeling at his feet, begging for his forgiveness.

He always looks down at me every time and says, "Get up, my sweet girl, you need not to cry or ask for my forgiveness. You were already forgiven when you stepped back onto my road. Now let's go. Let's keep walking. I told you I would never leave you or forsake you unlike man's world." One of the most powerful and lifechanging things he told as we walked down his road was that people on earth use the word "crazy" not in reference to a mental condition, but instead, they use it as a label for people and things they do not understand. And for the first time in my life, I felt like it was okay to just be me. Those words I carry in my heart every day, and I now know I am not the label that people have put on me, like a tattoo on my forehead. I am not crazy, and you or anyone else does not have the right to brand me that way. Just because I am different, it does not make me wrong nor does it make you right. I no longer listen to the white noise of the human kind. I only listen to the words of those that reach out to me in pain and don't know where to turn and, of course, the words spoken to me by the Lord Almighty that has set me free. I now am my own best friend, and I only truly trust 100 percent the word of God. After all, if God be for me, then who dare be against me?

The Lord told me, "Now that I have freed you from the bondage of the world and the wicked, now you will go forth and help only those that come to you. I will send them to you by way of your glowing spirit, a spirit only the condemned can see. They will not know you but will see your light. When they come, you stop what you're doing and listen to their cries. The Holy Ghost will guide you as to what to say and do. But your understanding, your kindness, and your touch will bring them back to life as I have brought you back to life. Deny not one as I have not denied you. Do not look at the flesh you see before you. But instead, look at the soul you see inside."

For several years now, that is exactly what has happened. Those that have nothing left, that feel written off by society, tortured in their minds, and suffered from addition find me, wherever I am. They never ask for anything; they just start talking, and I know what they need. I know what they are looking for. I see the pain in their eyes, like a mirror staring back at me. I feel their condemnation and rejection from their families and from society. I speak the words out of my mouth that are not my own, and then I hug them or hold their hand. They always say, "Thank you." I say, "Do not thank me. Your thanks belong to the Lord. I am only a living vessel he works through." Tears run down their face, and wholeness is restored in my heart. I could never restore my own personal self or bring back my family or the children that don't want me in their lives even though I almost killed myself trying. But each time someone in need comes to me, I feel like I am no longer worthless, no longer condemned; and for a few moments, I feel as though I do belong and are accepted by them and by God.

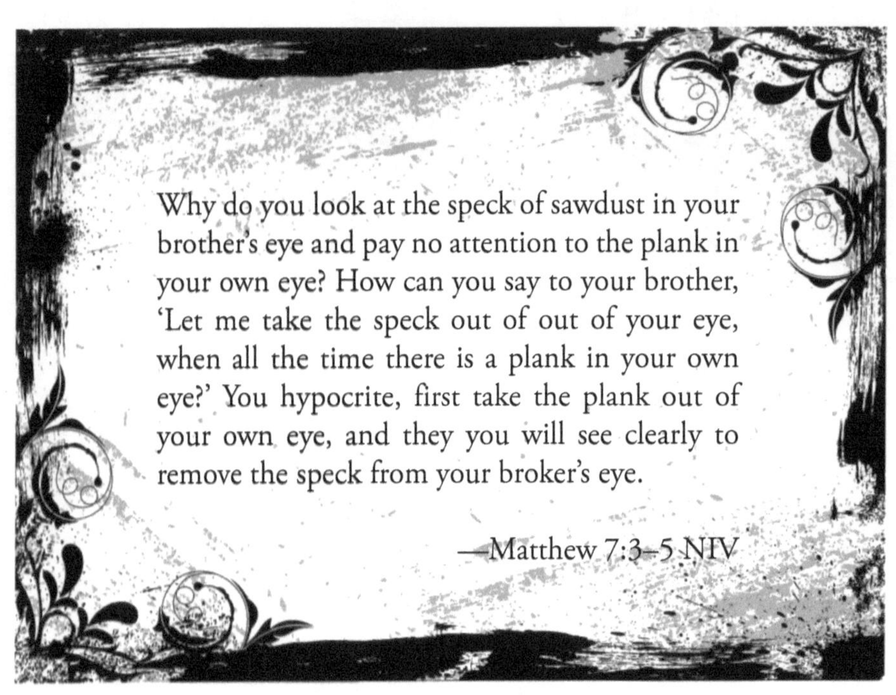

Why do you look at the speck of sawdust in your brother's eye and pay no attention to the plank in your own eye? How can you say to your brother, 'Let me take the speck out of out of your eye, when all the time there is a plank in your own eye?' You hypocrite, first take the plank out of your own eye, and they you will see clearly to remove the speck from your broker's eye.

—Matthew 7:3–5 NIV

CHAPTER 10

The Apology

In life, we all make choices we later regret. Some of us, more than others. We make decisions based on how we feel at that very moment. We harbor resentments, and we make bad judgement calls that sooner or later we wish we had not. The word apology simply means "a regretful acknowledgment of an offense or failure." What separates us from being human and not animals is that 99 percent of us are not narcissistic and truly do have emotional feelings and connections to people we cannot forget. Carrying around the burden of regret or forgiveness you yourself want is something suicides are made of. How many times have we all thought, *I wish I could go back and tell that person I was sorry and maybe it would have made a difference, and just maybe they would still be here today.* Every thirty seconds in this world, someone attempts to take their own life. The truth is, someone in that state of mind is not based on one simple apology; it's based on many. Usually from multiple people thinking they will punish you by not offering forgiveness or even saying the basic statement of "I messed up, I was wrong." But most of society does not think that way until after the person is already dead. And if you think for one second that you did not have a part in that person's decision to end their life, you are very wrong. If you held on to the apology they wanted so badly or the forgiveness they wanted to hear from you, that you just would not give, then yes you do hold a piece of the blame. Much like a poker game, so is suicide. You must have a full house of the same kind to dominate the win. Though as rare as a successful suicide is, versus the millions of attempts that are made, you still must be holding a royal flush and the perfect storm has to align of pain, rejection, hopelessness, and betrayal; all at the same time for this to occur. Don't ever think you could have done nothing, because deep down inside yourself, you know you could have! But instead to save face and to go on living your pitiful life, you tell yourself and others, "No one could have changed the outcome." Good luck living with that in your mind and heart the rest of your days. Then later, explaining that to God on your judgement day; why you did nothing, but could have.

I know this, because I have seen it myself personally, and still live it today. It was never your right to punish that person anyways regardless of what they had done. That is the job of the one we call "God." The difference between "mercy and forgiveness" is the same outcome, but the reasoning behind why you are giving it is different. Forgiveness is for the victim to be set free, not for the offender. Mercy is to be given to those that don't deserve it but ask for it. As a believer in God and a follower of Christ, we are commanded to "forgive our trespasses as though we forgive those that trespass against us." Why do we have to let it get to this point? Why do people think they are so special and so important that they don't have to offer or accept an apology of any kind? In case you don't know or perhaps you're not sure, let me tell you loud and clear: you are not any more special than anyone else here on this earth nor does the world revolve around you! We are all the same in this world, rich, poor, man, woman, race, intelligence level, etc. We all came into this world the same, with nothing, and we will all leave the same exact way we came in. Denying someone the right to be free on the inside is a mortal crime that you will pay for it eventually and eternally until you decide to finally do the right thing no matter what it costs you. But in most cases, it is just too little and much too late.

I don't know anyone that claims to be a "Christian," a follower of Jesus Christ, that does not understand exactly what the Bible says about forgiveness, repentance, and making amends. How can anyone possibly show their face at a church or post "holy" scriptures from the Bible on their social media page that says, "Every day is new day to for a new beginning in Jesus Christ," or anything even remotely close to that, and then have a picture of your own self right next to the clouds of heaven and not practice what you say you stand for and believe in? How does that work? How do you not have guilt inside and how are you not ashamed of yourself? Are you that vain or narcissistic or even psychotic? Well, two out of those three are actually forms of mental disorders. Maybe it's you that should be examined and evaluated by a psychiatrist. At least I can be open and honest about the fact that I have *never* been forced to seek psychiatric care. I have done it all on my own for twenty-two years now, and I continuously fight the battle with The Monster every day.

However, the difference between me and you is that I admit I have issues, take psychiatric medications, get therapy, and don't lie to people about who I really am. At the very least, I am true to God, true to myself, and true to others whether they like or want to even hear it. I don't hide behind a bible and use it as a shield in order to throw stones at others or, even worse, use it to hide behind in order to not see or have to deal with what is really going on in and around you. Nothing outrages me more than a lying self-proclaimed "religious person" from whatever order or denomination that believes in God but does the exact opposite of what his word says.

People nowadays value, take pride in, and measure their confidence and self-worth based on how many friends they have that are listed on social media accounts, which, by my personal opinion, is totally stupid by any standard. Most of those people that participate in that crap are just posting and painting everyone a picture about how happy and fabulous their lives, marriage, kids, and careers are. But what you don't see them post is the ugly truth. The reality is that their kids are in and out of jail, have drug and alcohol addiction problems, their marriage is falling apart, they lost their jobs, the bank is now foreclosing on their half a million-dollar home, they are hiding their $50,000 car around the street corner—trying to keep it from getting repossessed—and they just came home today to a disconnection notice on their front door from the electric company. Now, that is shit you will never see posted but what is truly going on.

My question is how many of those people do you really think would immediately come to your side when a crisis or real tragedy happens to you? I don't mean their posts of promised prayers. I mean actually show the hell up at where you are at when you actually need them? I can honestly tell you not many, not even one.

I chose not to participate anymore with fake ass online postings and bullshit statements with happy pictures of perfect lives that just don't really exist. If I feel I want someone to blow smoke up my ass, then trust me, I know just who to pick up the phone and call. Luckily, I don't need to go online and watch hundreds of postings every day of people more troubled than I nor do I put on this mask of perfection and then try to prove it's real by posting a picture that corresponds to the lie they want you to believe. Whatever happened to personal connection? What happened to going to visit someone and talking face to face or picking up the phone calling them directly? That way, you can see in their eyes or hear in their voice what the truth is. Whether it be good or bad, at least you know and are not deceived. You may be thinking to yourself that I am filled with hatred, rage, and resentfulness, and you know what, your damn right I am. I don't know any human being that can go through the hell I went through and still go through today, lose everything they got including their kids, spouses, homes, money, cars, careers, so-called friends, and even most of their family members, and battle a mental condition all at the same time. And that would not do or make the same choices I did to get to where I am today. And the only way I can let go of it in a healthy way now and not physically hurt myself or anyone else is if I open my mouth and find my voice, that was once silenced, and speak loud and clear with the truth.

The words you don't want to hear or accept as the truth. The shameful reality that you don't want people to know. The true, heartfelt apology you won't give to me. I am sick and tired of always being the one to beg for forgiveness, wipe someone's ass, and pretend that yes, it was all my fault; everything is always my fault, and no one else but me to blame because I am the one with the official diagnosis of mental illness in order to get let back into the circle when all of it is a bullshit lie in order to keep peace or have somewhere, some family to belong to. I will no longer accept the blame for anything that I know for a fact I am not guilty of just so I can be accepted and not black-balled or shunned. If you are not strong enough as a person to be able to accept even some blame to any situation that went wrong that you were involved in, then that is your problem not mine, and I no longer give a damn that you don't want to hear or see the truth. I refuse to participate or be a part of a family, a friendship, or a relationship that exists and resides on a foundation of a house of lies. I no longer care if I am not accepted or welcomed because I speak the truth, own up to my wrongdoings, and make conscious effort to fix what I destroyed or what someone destroyed in me. I have learned that if I am right and feel it in my gut, then I am right; but if I am wrong, then I am wrong. And me and only me can make it right. And most importantly, if I am right with God and he has told or showed me so, then I no longer care if I am right with you or any other human on this earth. Nor does your apology really even matter anymore.

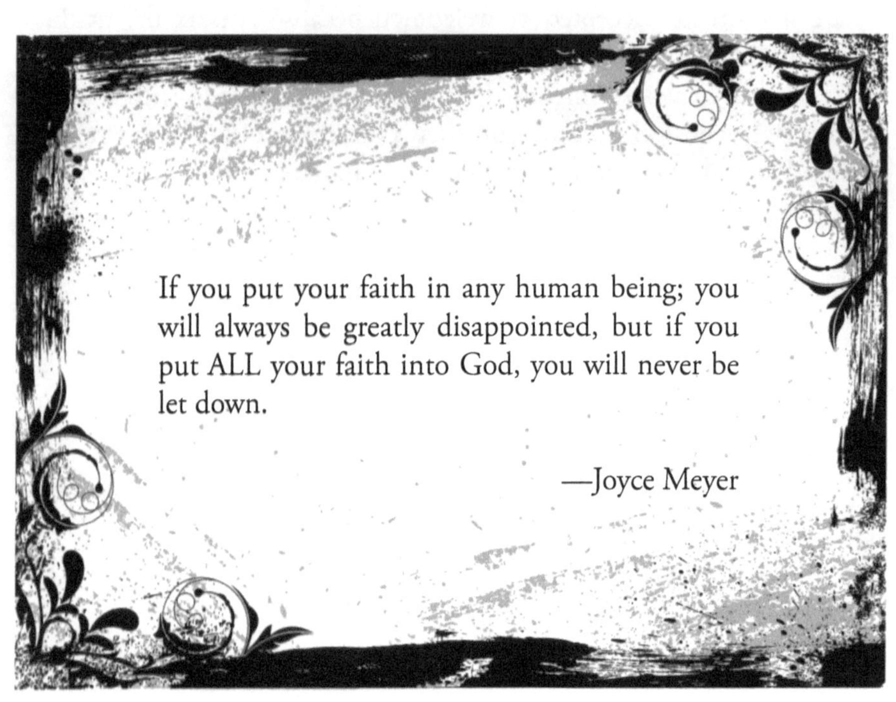

If you put your faith in any human being; you will always be greatly disappointed, but if you put ALL your faith into God, you will never be let down.

—Joyce Meyer

CHAPTER 11

Who Is Really to Blame?

Blame and accountability are two things that no one at first wants to claim responsibility for. When someone is "called out" on the outcome of their actions, words, or behaviors that have resulted in the hurt, destruction, devastation, or death, the instant human reaction is, "Well, I didn't do it!" They never even stop for one second to think of what their own part might have been in it. They just instantly reply like a little child who spilled the milk all over the floor; they run, they don't try to clean it up, and they just take off, leaving the mess for someone else to clean up. But just like adults, children don't think of the domino effect they have now set into place by not just cleaning up their own mess and admitting to it. Not only did they spill the milk on the floor, made a huge puddle, ran off, and left it there because they were scared to get into trouble, then someone unknowingly comes into the kitchen soon after, slips, and falls in the mess and now has a broken arm, leg or is seriously hurt. For children, this kind of behavior and negligence is not surprising, but for adults, it's totally unacceptable.

For example, it's quitting time a long stressful workday is now over, so you stop by the bar or local pub after work having a few drinks with friends and coworkers. Before you know, it's around eight or nine o'clock and dark outside. You take your usual route home, but because it is dark and your brain reacts much slower now after all the cocktails with your buddies, you think you see a dog or animal jump out of nowhere and you hit it. Your windshield is covered in blood, and your front bumper is dented in. You stop and get out of the car to see what is was. You soon realize it was actually a person a human being walking on the side of the road and not an animal. You don't know if they are alive or dead. You begin to have racing thoughts through your mind like, *If I call the police or ambulance, I will lose everything including my spouse, my kids, my job, and depending on if the person is already dead or not, I will spend the rest of my life in prison all because I had a few innocent drinks with my friends.*

You begin to justify in your mind reasons as why you should get back in your car and drive off and not do anything because in your mind, it was an accident; you are not a murderer or a violent person. Why should I have to pay such severe consequences? You then look around and see no cars, no witnesses, and it's dark outside on heavily wooded, winding roads. You make the decision that will haunt you the rest of your life. You quickly get back in the car, speed off, make it home, hose off your car, then you go to the nearest pay phone to call anonymously to report seeing someone hurt on the road and hang up. You go home and go to bed, wake up the next morning, and see on the news that a single mother of four was hit by a car last night as she was walking home from work and later died at the hospital from her injuries. And the doctors who tried to save her said if she had gotten to the hospital way earlier than she did, she would probably be still alive today, but she had lost too much blood by the time they got her. You now are overwhelmed by guilt. If you hadn't been so worried about yourself, this single mother of four would still be alive. Yes, it was an accident because you did not mean to hit her. You could have just as easily hit her on your way home sober. However, your wrong split-second decision caused a huge domino effect that you can now do nothing about. The whole reason for these two stories is this: it can be something as simple as spilled milk that someone gets hurt or as bad as hitting someone with their car after drinking and leaving them to die. Both were not done intentionally, but both the injury and the death could have been avoided just by stopping and saying, "I did it. I am sorry. It wasn't intentional, but I will now clean up my own mess before things get worse and someone is permanently hurt or killed by my mistakes. But now the damage is done, and you can't just go back and change it."

By the way, both of these stories I just told are 100 percent true and really did happen. They just did not happen to me, thank God. Probably one of the saddest, most unfair, true stories I know about that still pulls at my heartstrings today and makes me say, "Who is really to blame?" is a story about a woman who married in the early fifties. She had the picture perfect "all-American" life we think of when we think of that time era. She had a great husband with a great job, they bought a nice home, had four kids, she was the stay-at-home mom with the white picket fence and all until one day, it all changed. Shortly after her fourth child was born, she started exhibiting strange behavior that was totally out of character for her. Her husband took her to the doctor, but the behavior continued to get worse and more erratic. At this time in history, psychiatric diagnoses were primitive, and so were their medications and methods of treatment. Her husband was finally told by the doctor that he believes she has developed full-blown schizophrenia, maybe induced or brought on chemically by the birth of the fourth child. He was told she will not get better and cannot even care for herself much less four small children. He said all that can be done is put her into a long-term asylum that deals with the mentally ill, and there she will be sedated and will not be a danger or risk to herself or to the children. The husband was devastated, but he had to think of the children first. The man had his wife legally committed to what was then called an, "insane asylum," today they call it "a behavioral health facility." So in the late fifties, the woman was locked up, sedated, and left there to live out the rest of her life. The husband felt he had no other choice but to divorce her and find a new wife because he needed a mother for his children. And that is what he did about a year and a half after committing his wife. The children were so young he thought it would be best to not talk about their birth mother and remove everything from the house including her personal items and pictures of her and claim his new wife as their mother. The four children were six years of age and under, so the children had no reason not to trust and believe what their father had told them. Only the oldest two remembered a different woman as their mother. As the years moved on, all the children had forgotten any memory of their birth mother. They all truly believed that this other woman was their mom, especially after the new wife and their father went on to add a new baby sibling into the home. Life for the new family of seven went on as normal. The woman in the asylum was never visited or talked about by her former husband or even her own family ever again. Because in that period of time, you were told by doctors and professionals: "You must commit them because they are never gonna get better, only worse over time. And that they are a danger to themselves and others, plus if you keep them in your home, they will require twenty-four-hour care, and everyone will know, and they will ostracize and shun you for having 'crazy' in your family! It is hard, but it is best for all involved to commit them and just move forward with your life and let them go. They are already gone in their minds." Which we know today is total bullshit, but you can chalk that up to ignorance and a lack in technology of the time era.

Now here is where this whole story takes a wild and interesting turn of events. So the woman spent three decades in that insane asylum ran by the same head doctor since the forties. He tried experimental treatments on the patients, like most doctors of psychiatry did in that day, like "electric shock therapy" and is known today as ECT and much less inhumane than what is was then. And they gave shock treatments to patients without needing a consent from anyone. Besides, these are people that their relatives gave to the state and said "Here ya go, good luck with them. They are all yours now." They gave it to patients that today would *never* even be a candidate for ECT. They just tried it on everyone in the hospital to see what might happen. They did not sedate the patients and, in most cases, didn't even strap them down. The nurses held them down while the doctor gave them electric shock to their brains multiple times with wattages that were way too high, in some cases, rendering the person totally catatonic or in a vegetable-like state afterward.

I can only imagine what this poor lady went through for almost thirty years. It wasn't until the early eighties that the head doctor of the asylum retired. But he first interviewed and found his replacement before he left. He chose a young doctor fresh out medical school with two years residency in psychiatry. The last thing he said to the new, young doctor was, "I know your new and full of all these ideas and possibilities they teach in psychiatry these days but let me save you the time, effort, and disappointment. These people that come through that door never come out alive or changed. Just run things the way I have it set up, and your life will be a lot easier than the forty-five years I spent here." The young doctor, of course did not listen to him, and besides, the new advancements in medication and research studies he had been taught and trained in was exactly what he was gonna do, along with the changes the world of psychology had started implementing with the changing of the name insane and asylum and make it now "mental hospitals."

He started by reevaluating each and every patient that was already admitted and did not accept any new patients until all seventy-five current patient cases were already done. He came across this lady committed in the fall of 1958. It was now 1982. He ran all the tests and x-rays possible at that time and reviewed her medical records, and something very interesting stuck out like a sore thumb to him about her. He saw on her head x-ray severely impacted wisdom teeth, so severe it would take serious surgery to get them out. But the young doctor had remembered that there is a ton of nerves running in your jaw line, especially in the back part of your mouth, and if those nerves are cut off, they affect an area of the brain that controls behavior, reaction, and sensibility. And if those nerves had been totally cut off from reaching the brain, you could exhibit "schizophrenic-type" behaviors, and it could have easily been misdiagnosed. So the young doctor scheduled a full day of surgery to have impacted wisdom teeth removed. About two days later while she was recovering, his hunch was right! She started slowly behaving different and asking a lot of questions, and one of them was, "Where am I? Where are my children?" He soon realized this lady never belonged in here at all and had been medically sedated and given inhumane treatments and experimental drugs for thirty years for a condition she did not even have.

The most devastating part was when he sat down with the her and explained what had happened, where she was, and how many decades had gone by—that she really had no idea of. He soon realized what he had done was ethically and morally right, but by looking at the reaction of the lady, whose life was stolen from her and the tears that ran down her face, he thought to himself, *Maybe I should have just left well-enough alone; maybe it would have been better for her not knowing.* But the damage had already been done. They released the lady soon after, and she went home to her family that didn't know her and most were dead, including her parents, and she then tried to reconnect with her children that were all grown-up and had their own families now, and they stared at a mother who they never knew existed. This is very sad but a true story which brings up the question: "Who is really to blame?" Was it the doctor who committed her in the fifties? Was is it her husband for agreeing and signing off on the order to put her away; followed by him quickly moving on and divorcing her and remarried starting a new life and convincing the children this new wife was their mother? Or was it her own family who let the shame of what other people would say or think if they chose to keep her with them? Or maybe it was the fault of the head doctor that ran the asylum for forty-five years that never bothered reevaluating the patients there and just used them to experiment on because he refused to believe these people would or could ever get better? The truth is all of them have a piece of the blame in destroying this woman's life. If even one of them had made a different choice, the outcome could have been very different. But like most situations, dealing with mental illness, addiction, or abuse, no one is ever held accountable for their part in contributing to the outcome.

My story is somewhat similar in the fact that everyone had a part in building who I am today, including myself, but no one, except my father, has ever truly apologized and tried to make amends to me. In any twelve-step program no matter what your addiction and/or mental illness was or is today, the message is still the same and is interpreted to me as this:

1. Admitting to one's self that you are powerless over your addiction and/or mental illness, and now because of that, your life has become unmanageable.

2. You came to believe that a power greater than our own self could restore you to sanity.
3. You have made a decision to turn your will and lives over to God as you understand him.
4. Make a fearless and moral inventory of oneself, being 100 percent truthful in all areas about the wrong you had done.
5. Admit to God, to yourself, and to another human being the exact nature of your own wrongdoings.
6. You are entirely ready for God to remove all defects of character.
7. Show total humility and humbly ask God to remove all of your shortcomings.
8. Make a list of people you had harmed or hurt and be willing to make amends to them all.
9. Make a direct amends to all people that are still alive and that you can find as long as your contacting them does not further hurt or injure them in any way regardless if they want to hear from you or not.
10. Continue to take a daily inventory of yourself and when you are wrong, you immediately admit to it and truly apologize and try to make things right if possible.
11. Pray and meditate every day to improve your spiritual connection with God, asking only from him to give you the knowledge and strength to carry out his plan for you today.
12. Now that you have done all these things, you are now a new person. Go and pass the message along to anyone who you see struggling with addiction and/or mental illness and live your life now the way you have been taught, never looking back at the person you buried back at step one and use these steps in everything you do from now on.

Having the knowledge of these steps, as well as working them all, makes me feel like I am a part of a very small but intelligent group of people that exists in this world today. And the one thing that completely outrages me more than anything in this world is ignorance. I could understand if this were fifty or hundred years ago and people did not have the open and free access to knowledge about anything at your fingertips, but today, you can go online and find anything you ever wanted to know about. You can get a college degree online. You can learn and physically watch from wherever you are on how to build a car engine completely from the start, or you can even watch brain surgery live from your bed. Why ignorance outrages me so bad is because of three simple things: (1) I was *never* allowed to live in or be ignorant about anything in life. God made sure I was taught the hard way about everything I know today whether I wanted to or not. (2) Now, you don't even have to know how to read in order to watch and learn anything online or simply turn on your television, so you don't get to use the excuse to say, "I didn't have access to know!" (3) You know all this information is available to you about mental illnesses including suicide, any type of addiction, and neglect or abuse, and you don't understand anything about these subjects, and you *still* choose not to educate your own self about it.

Wow, I would be ashamed to open my mouth and say anything to anyone about a pain or a claimed hurt or struggle they say they are going through if I did not have all the facts first! I would never argue or debate with a professional mechanic of twenty-five years or the engineer that designed my car about what I thought was wrong with it or how to fix it because I have no clue what I am talking about. I may have general knowledge of it based solely on the sound it makes or a similar problem I have experienced in the past that I have had to deal with a former car I once owned making the same noise, but that is where I stop because I know I have no idea or the education of what I am talking about. Now the experienced mechanic or engineer may tell me key points as to what they think or know what the problem is, and I can then go online and research what they have said if I am really interested or truly want to know; but that still does not make me an expert, and I still am not going to look stupid as hell and try to debate about it with them. Bottom line is, if you don't know all possible sides of something someone went through or you have done absolutely nothing to educate yourself on the subject or subjects a claimed "loved one" is experiencing or suffering from, then keep your mouth shut until you do and *never assume anything*!

Gossip and confrontation about a subject you have never personally went through or lived is totally "stupid" on your part, and that is exactly how you will look when you decide you're going to go up against someone who has so save yourself the embarrassment and use your two ears to listen and your one mouth to keep closed until you do know all the facts. That brings up the million-dollar question of "who is really to blame" for what has happened to me in my life from birth till now? Who's influence on me as a child all the way up till age eighteen impacted me so greatly that I never felt I had a choice or that I even had the option of using my own voice in this the world until I was thirty-three? Who should I thank for building the foundation in which my life sits on this very day at forty? Was it my teenage mother who I felt little connection with that ignored me and all the warning signs of mental illness in my brain and my actions which caused me to not seek out real professional help until I was eighteen years of age and an adult? Or was it my severely mentally ill father that everyone wrote off and said, "he chooses to be the way he is?" Maybe it was the fact of, at ten years old, I lost the twenty-four-year old man that took over the role as being my "stand-in father" that shot himself in the head purposely, leaving this world and me behind? It might have been the woman I consider to be my real mother but was actually my grandmother who also chose suicide but a much slower one and died when I was nineteen of smoking herself to death, when she was only in her fifties? Or could it possibly be all the broken relationships and marriages I had went through or that I lost custody of one of my children at two years of age and the other at just six months because I was considered to have a "chronic disease" that has no cure or where certain stability was unknown at any time? Was it all the people who ever walked through my life that consistently said "I was crazy" but did nothing to help me or change my situation other than letting me know their uneducated opinion? Or, last but not least, does all the blame just need to be put solely on me for both my actions and reactions to situations in life as both a child, adolescent, teenager, and an adult?

The truth and the real answer to that million-dollar question is all of the above. But the devastating reality of it all to me is, the only one who was held accountable for their actions and bad decisions was me. I am currently serving my second life sentence with no possibility of parole, in a prison I built for myself to live in my own home that nobody but me and God can see or feel. So what I want say to all those I have ever hurt or disappointed unintentionally or intentionally: I am telling you directly right now; I will give you today, what has only ever been given to me by my father; I am truly sorry for any and all things I have ever done that hurt or damaged your soul to what you thought was unrepairable. This, my dear, is something you believed you would never hear from me. But you were wrong. You just did. I know, and I am well aware of what I did, and you know exactly who you are, and I am sorry and I hope that one day, you are able to forgive me and also offer me your forgiveness in return and finally a *truthful*, heartfelt apology like the one I just gave you. I have shown and told any and all that read this book that I have humility.

But the question that remains is, do you? Are you truly brave enough to only tell me and maybe a handful or less that you were wrong and that you were truly sorry to me when I am telling and writing it down for the whole world to see? Only time will reveal that, but my educated guess based on past history tells me that you will not, and I will die never hearing or seeing forgiveness or apologies that I deserved.

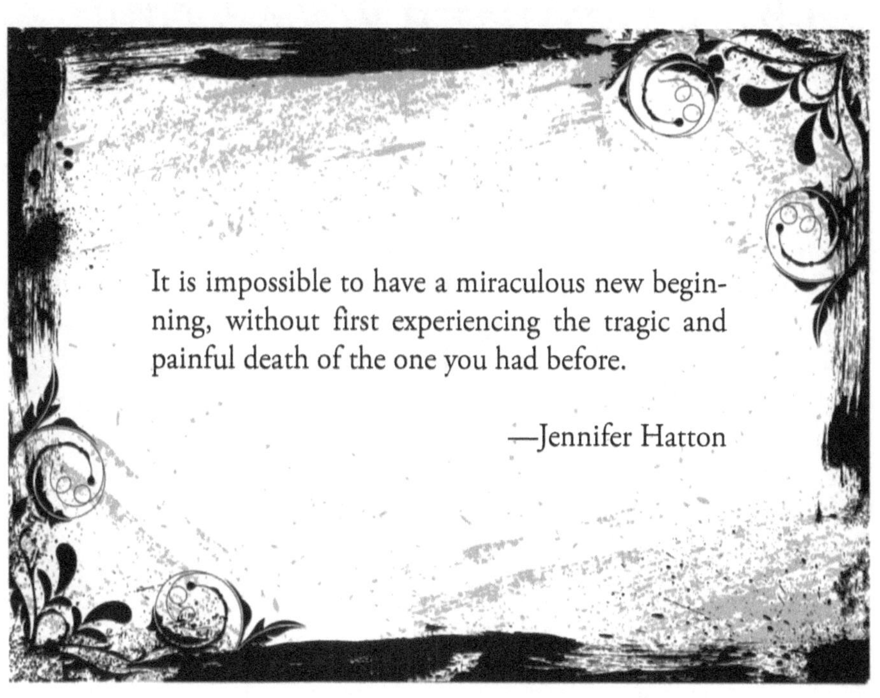

It is impossible to have a miraculous new beginning, without first experiencing the tragic and
painful death of the one you had before.

—Jennifer Hatton

CHAPTER 12

The Beginning or the End?

Faith and hope go hand in hand. One cannot exist without the other. Just like the human body cannot physically exist without both a brain and a heart. Both have extremely important jobs they do, and both fuel each other. But when it comes to actions and behaviors in people, it is a different story. People are only led by one of two things: good or evil. You cannot be led by both at the same time. Everything you do or say is powered by one of those two intentions. And any action you take in this world that is led by evil will never prosper in the end. Life is about consistent growth, not continuous death. Evil intentions will make you to stand still and will eventually cause you to move backward in life.

Having mental illness causes this borderline we walk between good and evil to be blurred. Much like if you have two shots of vodka the line you walk begins to be slightly fuzzy, but if you have ten shots the line becomes so blurred you can no longer see it. Having any diagnosis of mental illness flips a switch in your brain, and you cannot see the pathway as sharp as "normal" people do. Then if you add in self-medicating that easily morphs into addiction, this line becomes almost impossible to see on your own. Being mentally ill is both a blessing and a curse. It is a blessing in the fact that you see things very different, more in depth, and are extremely sensitive to what is going on or around you. Whereas most people don't even pay attention or look close enough to see those fine lines. But like the old saying, "The devil is in the details." Those plagued with this chronic disease, notice these things in true depth and vivid color way more than the normal society can imagine. Those that claim to be normal are incapable of seeing at first glance what is outside the picture frame. They only see what is inside the frame, and most of them simply just don't care to see anything else. It's only after these details add up to something, way bigger than the action itself, can the ignorant finally understand what we see; and then they try to go back and fix from day one, which as everyone knows, sometimes is just too little and much too late. When a loved one commits suicide, it is then that the normal person says, "I had no idea that things were that bad. I never noticed the signs." It is only when the dawn comes that we remember the darkness. And it is only when we face death that we remember how precious that human life truly was.

Some people, no matter what I do, say, or accomplish in this life will always think of and label me as "crazy" and as a "drunk." They will let biological disease and extremely unfortunate circumstances that happened to me and that were not my fault and blamed me for the reaction I made to devastation, overshadow who I really am, who I could have been, or the message I fought so hard to get out to save others from the fate I lived. They will never really know how much I have truly suffered and will refuse to see or acknowledge the changes I have made in my own life and in the lives of others. Or the good mother I tried and desperately wanted to be, but that option was taken away from me, and because of it, I don't honestly know how to mother my children.

The one that suffered the most from this was my son. Today he hates me, and I have not seen or spoken to him in over a year. Not for my lack of trying but because he has a distorted vision in his mind of me that several grown adults put there for as long as he can remember. That coupled with my own feelings of inadequacy of not knowing how to be there for him, the guilt and shame I felt that he deserved better but I could not provide. What he doesn't know is that I truly love him and would give him anything I could or had or ever would have, even my own life, if it would repair everything for him. I pray to God that one day, he finds out the truth and comes back to me and wants to be a part of my life; but if it is not God's will, then I pray that he will be blessed with a better life than the one I had. And yes, I do take responsibility for the pain I have caused him. Unfortunately, he doesn't know about the empty, painful holes family, friends, and former husbands caused me or allowed to happen to me that still exists today in my heart from the devastating rejections and knives in my back. Holes and emptiness of a life I lost that today are now being filled with the happiness I feel when I can bring a smile to someone's face that had lost all hope and faith in this world.

Ironically, after all the things I have done and said that they say are "completely unforgivable" no matter what and they write me off as though I was dead or a bad business venture gone wrong, the reality is that if it came out that I was actually diagnosed with Alzheimer's disease or dementia, they would all suddenly change their mind. They would say things like, "Oh, that explains everything." And easily forgive and forget all that had happened and accept me, welcome me back home, and say to everyone, "It was never her fault. She has a terrible disease that robs her of thinking clearly. Therefore, we have to let all her actions and behaviors go." Alzheimer's and dementia are accepted in today's society, but any form of mental illness is not. I ask, "How is it any different?" I never asked for this disease. I never made any health-related choices to cause it. But I am still today held to the standards of a modern-day criminal and ostracized by most of my family and now my teenage son. Each day I die a little more inside, waiting for a God to save me that some say does not even exist, but I know different. I know the Lord, and he loves me. However, there are also those that would tell you a totally different opinion about me. They would say that I was a bright light in a very dark place, and that they will always remember the kindness, understanding, and acceptance I showed them, no matter who they were or what kind of life they came from. That is why I now give back the gavel and long robe to the God Almighty and live by his judgement and approval because in the end, he is the only one that truly matters.

This book has been the true story of my journey in life with mental illness, self-medication that led to addiction, bad choices, and plain devastation. To keep the open, honesty, and truthfulness I promised from the beginning of how I really feel inside, I must tell you that if I had a choice to go back and relive it again, I would not. Not every story has a happy ending. Not every life is precious to someone. And if I knew what I know today and could go back to day the I realized I was different from everyone else as a child, I would have say that I would have chosen to end it there and go home to where I could consistently exist in peace with the God who made me and knows that I'm special, believes in me, and sees my heart of gold and never look back.

None of this life was worth the extreme price I had to pay in order to live it. If life had a light switch, I would have turned it off decades ago. So the true and final question to be answered is, "Is this the end of the beginning or the beginning of the end?" The answer to that question is not held by anyone living on this earth. What I do know is when we are born, we are already equipped with an internal hourglass built inside us with only so many grains of sand. Some have millions of grains and will live to be a hundred, but others are born with only few grains in their glass and the beginning becomes the end before the first breath.

In a perfect world, I would save everyone. I would find the strength within myself to defeat The Monster forever in anyone's mind that suffers his presence. But in the "real world," the very best I can do is to hope and pray that I can at least save a few for the outcome of life that was worse than my own. The best words I can possibly tell you are the ones I didn't have to say, the ones you can now see inside your own self.

Today I no longer care that the world misjudges me or that I really have no family to call my own. I now live to open the eyes of those that call themselves "normal" and believe that they "know it all" when really they are extremely ignorant and know nothing. I pray for them never to be judged and sentenced to death like myself and millions of other people just like me who battle The Monster inside their minds. I feel as though I was crucified for just trying to be me and my authentic self. Unfortunately, humankind does not like or accept those that go astray from the herd. Those that dare to step outside the box and be different. My advice to those that identify with me, my life, my struggles, my pain, and my nonacceptance by this world would be: keep fighting, keep loving, keep helping, keep believing, and for the sake of God, be who he made you to be—perfect just the way you are!

Jennifer Hatton has been known by many names over the years, throughout her several broken marriages and her lost identity. As long as she can remember, she was plagued by mental illnesses, disorders, and terrorized by the one she calls "The Monster." She wore a mask for decades, all to gain acceptance from the ones she thought loved her. She never found her authentic self until she finally walked out of the shadows and pulled off her mask. Only after that did she discover that it didn't matter who she pretended to be; those she loved and trusted most walked away and betrayed her anyways. Her whole life, "The Monster" spoke to her inside her mind, telling her she was not special, she was nothing, and that she was worthless. As a child, all the way to adulthood, she tried to reach out to the one's closest to her and tell them about the hell locked inside her mind. She was quickly shut down and told never to speak of him again. Or she would be branded for life. Her story represents the reality of millions of people all over the world that are forced to be silenced and hide in the darkness to avoid persecution and judgement from those that call themselves, "the normal society." Suicidal thoughts and actions took over her life, then the lives of those she loved and desperately tried to save, but could not. Today, she spends her life fighting for a cause that little seem to care about, but all are affected by as suicide rates continue to skyrocket all around the world, but is still considered a dirty secret, best kept in the dark.